Andrew Foyle is a solicitor advocate and the Head of Litigation for Scotland at Shoosmiths LLP, with over 17 year's experience advising and representing financial institutions and insolvency practitioners at all levels of the Court system in Scotland. His experience in the financial sector involves both pursuing and defending claims, including secured and unsecured asset/credit recovery, regulatory issues, mis-selling claims, fraud, negligence and contractual claims. He has been involved in a number of recent high profile cases in the banking sphere and has spent periods on secondment with two major clearing banks.

A Practical Guide to the Law of Spousal Guarantees in Scotland

A Practical Guide to the Law of Spousal Guarantees in Scotland

Andrew Foyle
LL.B. (Hons), LL.M., Dip LP, NP,
Solicitor Advocate
Partner in Commercial Litigation at Shoosmiths LLP, Edinburgh

Law Brief Publishing

Published 2021 by Law Brief Publishing, an imprint of Law Brief Publishing Ltd
30 The Parks
Minehead
Somerset
TA24 8BT

www.lawbriefpublishing.com

Paperback: 978-1-913715-46-5

Dedicated to the memory of

the late Ruari MacNeill

PREFACE

At the start of my traineeship in the Banking Litigation Team I was handed a voluminous file and asked to read into it in advance of sitting in on a consultation with counsel. It was my first exposure to the principle in Smith, but certainly not my last. I will not name the case, but it is one of those examined in this book. For the following couple of years the firm I trained with dealt with case after case where the principle was raised, and I was exposed to a number of examples, both reported and unreported, which helped shaped the law as it stands today.

I was fortunate enough to be trained in a firm which was at the vanguard in the development of this area of law. Ruari MacNeill (sadly no longer with us, but to whose memory this book is dedicated and for whom I worked for over a decade) together with my former colleague Claire Martin (my mentor as a trainee) were excellent teachers. Whilst there have been individual academic articles as new cases were reported, it has long been an ambition of mine to put all of my acquired knowledge on this area of law down in writing, so that it can be found in one place. I must thank Law Brief Publishing for allowing me to do so.

As we shall see, many of the big questions were settled some time ago. The subject is of more than academic interest however, and indeed it was only recently that the first successful case (since Smith) of a spouse challenging a standard security was heard in Scotland. The principles are therefore as important now as they were in 1997 and the most recent case law shows quite clearly that lenders cannot afford to be complacent. As you will read in the final chapter of this book, I foresee further litigation ahead. That is especially so given the unusual circumstances we are experiencing at the time of writing, which has led to an explosion of lending to businesses. Much of that lending is government-backed, but for those loans which are not, the probability of undue influence or fraud becoming a factor when lending is being arranged remotely cannot be underestimated.

There are many people I should thank. Ruari and Claire I have mentioned already, and without them I would never have been exposed to this area of law nor would I have had the opportunity to think about it so deeply. I have also mentioned, and would like to thank, Law Brief Publishing for asking me to write this, and for the support given during the writing process. We did not know at the time how bizarre 2020 would turn out to be. Having a project (and deadline) to occupy my mind outside of work has been immensely beneficial. I can't recommend the process enough!

Most importantly, however, I must thank my wife and children for allowing me the time, peace and quiet to undertake this writing during what would normally have been family time. One of the few upsides of the global pandemic was that I spent far more time at home and, if it were possible, got to appreciate my family more than ever.

As always, any errors in this book are entirely my own. The law is stated as at 1st January 2021.

Andrew Foyle
January 2021

CONTENTS

CHAPTER ONE

INTRODUCTION

The first thing to say about the law of spousal guarantees in Scotland is that, strictly speaking, it does not necessarily apply only to spouses. The principles which we shall examine in this work have been argued to apply to parents and children, cohabitants and indeed to employer / employee relationships. There have been varying degrees of success with some of these arguments, but the key point is that it is the nature of the relationship which is important and not the terminology. Put shortly it is about the balance of power, and the degree of thrall which one party may hold over another.

Having said all of that, it is an undeniable fact that the vast majority of claims have involved the granting of guarantees or cautionary obligations by one spouse (usually a wife) in relation to the debts of a business owned or operated by the other. Indeed the law is rooted in what has memorably been described in multiple cases as the laws "tender treatment of wives". In the modern era that phrase may seem patriarchal, and to this writer's knowledge this characterisation has been criticised by at least one senior female member of the judiciary, but it remains a remarkably stubborn soundbite to shake off.

Nevertheless it is worthwhile noting that the cornerstone of the principle – at least insofar as Scotland is concerned – is rooted in the principle of good faith and not in the marriage vows. It applies wherever there is a risk that consent to a personal guarantee or other cautionary obligation may be vitiated by reason of the relationship between the borrower and the guarantor.

As we shall examine, the law as it currently stands was a blatant example of judicial activism. The House of Lords deliberately extended the law in both England and Scotland in order to provide additional protection to spouses who were granting guarantees or securities in favour their spouse's business. The intention was to put more of the onus on lenders to ensure that the consent of their guarantors was freely given and fully understood.

The reasoning for that extension of the law will be examined in more detail below. It is worth noting at this juncture that whilst it was apparently the House of Lords' intention to have a degree of consistency on both sides of the border, subsequent Scottish decisions have diverged in a number of material respects from their English counterparts. As a result, the law of England and Wales in this area is significantly different in a number of aspects from the law of Scotland.

The law of England and Wales will be considered in this book, but it should be noted that the writer is not an English qualified lawyer and that nothing which is said about the law of England is intended to provide a definitive statement of the law south of the border. Rather, it is important to understand how the law of England developed in order to understand the state of play when the House of Lords came to hear the case of *Smith -v- Bank of Scotland* back in 1997. It is also instructive to contrast the subsequent divergence of the Scottish case law from the more prescriptive regime set out in the English cases.

After an initial flurry of cases in the late 1990's and early 2000's, the law in Scotland has since reached an equilibrium. The issue still arises, but with less frequency than before, and some of the attempts to extend the principles to other types of relationship seen in England have not (yet) materialised in Scotland. Whilst it may seem that most of the big issues have been settled, there is still scope for further litigation in this area as we shall consider at the end of this book.

This book is intended to be a practical guide for legal practitioners who may not be familiar with this highly specialist area of law. It is comprehensive in the sense that it examines the major case law in some detail, but is designed to be user-friendly and logical in its layout rather than purely academic.

Throughout this work we talk of "guarantors" and "guarantees", as well as of cautionary obligations. Whilst the law of cautionary is technically wider than merely the granting of personal guarantees, a full examination of the differences is beyond the scope of this book. Where differentiation is required between the two terms in order to aid understanding, a definition of the obligation is given. Beyond that, nothing turns on the use of one term or the other. The English legal term "surety" is used when discussing the English authorities, and (subject again to the caveat that the writer is not English qualified) is understood to be broadly equivalent to a cautionary obligation under Scots law.

CHAPTER TWO

THE LAW PRIOR TO 1997

The heart of this work concerns the duties which are incumbent upon a lender where they take a guarantee or other security from a third party for the debts of a business or person closely connected to that party.

The law of Scotland had been remarkably stable in this area for around 100 years until the *Smith* case came before the House of Lords in 1997. Indeed, for cases where what we shall refer to as "the *Smith* Principle" is not engaged, the position remains reasonably straightforward.

The law is helpfully encapsulated in the case of *Young -v- Clydesdale Bank.*[1]

Mr David Young, the pursuer in that action, was brother to a cattle salesman, Robert Young. Robert Young appears to have been in the habit of asking his brother to guarantee his debts to the bank, usually limited in amount to between £300 and £400. In due course, the pursuer was asked by his brother to sign (and did sign) a letter of guarantee which was unlimited in amount. He claimed that he was unaware of the unlimited nature of the guarantee and that he understood at the time of signing that the document amounted to a liability similar in amount to what he had given before – i.e. under £500.

Upon receiving a demand from the bank seeking payment of £5,000, the pursuer raised an action seeking reduction of the letter of guarantee. He brought three distinct arguments to bear:

1. He had signed the letter in the belief that his liability was to be limited in a similar way to his previous letters, and alleged that a

[1] (1889) 17 R 231

bank official had told him, "fraudulently", that the granting of the letter was a "mere matter of form".

2. That there was a duty upon the bank at the time of signature to inform him that his brother's account with the bank was overdrawn by £5,000, and that concealment of this fact from him amounted to fraud.

3. That he was under an essential error by reason of not being told that the overdraft stood at that amount and that the letter was unlimited in amount, and whether or not that error was induced by the bank, his signature had been applied under essential error as to the nature and effect of the document and he should be entitled to reduction of the document on that basis.

On the evidence, it appears that any misrepresentation as to the contents of the document originated with the guarantor's brother and his staff and not with the bank. It was a matter of admission that the document was not read before signature, and that Mr Young had not asked to read it "because [he] was under the idea that I knew what I was going to sign for before I went to the bank".[2] The question was, therefore, the extent to which the bank required to explain the terms of the document which the guarantor was signing and the liabilities to which he was exposing himself.

Unsuccessful at first instance, Mr Young reclaimed to the Inner House. In their judgment, the Inner House had no doubt that Mr Young and his co-cautioner Mr Mathieson had signed the document without any knowledge of its contents. They were also satisfied that the bank had neither offered nor insisted in reading over the document and/or explaining its contents. It was accepted that had the pursuer been aware of the true nature of the document he would not have signed it, and that he had been deceived as to the contents of the document by his brother.

[2] *Ibid* at p. 234

However, the issue in question was not resolved by the establishment of those facts.

The ratio of the case is helpfully encapsulated in the following paragraph:

> "If David Young, relying upon his brother's statement, chose to sign the document without reading, or without looking at what he was signing in order to ascertain what was in it, the consequences must fall upon himself, the bank believing—as they were entitled to believe—that the cautioner knew perfectly well what he was signing. They gave their money on the faith of this document, and it appears to me that that being so, the bank was not and could not be affected by any fraud, or undue concealment in this matter, as far as I can see. Having given money on the faith of the document that had been signed by David Young, David Young must be responsible for the amount."[3]

In relation to the duties incumbent upon the bank, and in particular whether the bank had a duty to disclose the extent of the principal debtor's indebtedness to the guarantor, the court commented that:

> "There can be no ground of complaint because of concealment by the bank-agent, for nothing is better settled than this, that a bank-agent is entitled to assume that the cautioner has informed himself upon the various matters material to the obligation he is about to undertake. The agent is not bound to volunteer any information or statement as to the accounts, although if information be asked he is bound to give it, and to give it truthfully."[4]

---

[3] *Ibid* at p.243, *per* Lord Adam

[4] *Ibid*, at p244, *per* Lord Shand

Thus, the *Young* case sets out very clearly the duties of the bank in circumstances where a guarantor was contemplating giving a guarantee for a relative's debts. Those duties can be summarised shortly:

- The bank had no duty to read the document to the guarantor nor to insist that they read it themselves.

- The bank had no duty to inform the guarantor of the state of the principal debtor's indebtedness.

- However, if asked a direct question in relation to the state of the debtor's account, the bank must answer honestly.

Beyond these duties, the risk lay upon the guarantor to satisfy themselves as to the obligations that they were undertaking and the degree of exposure which they might have. The only exception to that rule might be if it were shown that the principal debtor who induced the signature through misrepresentation was acting as agent for the lender, which would require specific factual averments.[5]

The issue of whether the lender has answered a question honestly will be a matter of fact, but might require more than merely giving a direct, narrow answer to a direct question. The lender may be required to elaborate on circumstances known to them which might affect the guarantor's decision to grant the guarantee. For example, a proposed guarantor asking if there was "any issue" with the debtor's application might require more than an answer in the negative in circumstances where there had been previous applications for credit which had been declined.[6]

The force of the principle that a lender is not required to disclose the state of the principal debtor's account was further demonstrated in *Royal*

[5] See the discussion in *Royal Bank of Scotland -v- Shanks* 1998 SLT 355

[6] See *Bank of Scotland -v- Forbes* 2011 GWD 12-270

Bank of Scotland -v- Greenshields[7] in which a customer of the bank with an overdraft of £300 and obligations under promissory notes of £1,100 requested a friend to grant a guarantee in his favour in the amount of £300. Believing the customer's indebtedness to amount to only £300 the proposed guarantor told the bank he was willing to guarantee £300. The bank advised him that a guarantee of £300 may not assist the debtor as the entire amount would be taken up by the bank. The guarantor was therefore persuaded to grant a guarantee for £500. At no point did he ask as to the state of the debtor's account, and nor was this information volunteered. The guarantor did ask whether the debtor's financial position was sound, which was answered in the affirmative.

In due course the debtor defaulted and the guarantee was called upon. The guarantor defended the bank's claim on the grounds that the bank ought to have corrected his misunderstanding of the true state of the debtor's account by disclosing that his borrowing was £1,100 and not £300. It was held that the bank had no such duty:

> "The only circumstances in which I can conceive that a duty of disclosure would emerge, and a failure to disclose would be fatal to the Bank's case, would be where a customer put a question or made an observation in the presence and hearing of the bank-agent which necessarily and inevitably would lead anyone to the conclusion that the intending guarantor was labouring under a misapprehension with regard to the state of the customer's indebtedness. Nothing short of that, in my opinion, would do."[8]

This general principle that an error induced either unilaterally or by a third party (even in cases of fraudulent misrepresentation) has no effect on the enforceability of the contract remains the law of Scotland in most commercial matters. In *Universal Import Export GmbH -v- Bank of Scotland*[9] for example the shoe was on the other foot, and it was the bank

---

7 1914 SC 259

8 *Ibid*, at p.268 *per* The Lord President

9 1994 SCLR 944

who sought to avoid payment of a bank draft which was said to have been issued pursuant to the fraudulent misrepresentation of the bank's customer. The payee under the draft was not a party to the fraud and sued for payment of the draft. It was held both at first instance and on appeal that the bank could not avoid liability on the basis of fraud by a third party.

Another example can be found in *Whiteaway Laidlaw Bank Ltd -v- Green*[10] where a company director who had signed a loan agreement containing a personal guarantee was not permitted to put a lender to proof on the question of whether one of his fellow directors (whom it was said misled him into signing the guarantee) had been an agent for the bank. The court cited *Young* as being conclusive on the point.

Where a lender makes honest representations to a cautioner but the facts change after signature of the guarantee, this may be excusable in certain circumstances. In *Bank of Ireland -v- Morton*[11] the guarantor sought reduction of his guarantee claiming that he had entered the guarantee under the apprehension that a first-ranked security over company property was also being taken by the lender. It appears that the lenders were under the same misapprehension and had communicated this to the guarantor. In fact, the security when it was granted was not first-ranked, which might have affected the guarantor's exposure. The Inner House of the Court of Session held that there was no duty upon the lender to inform the guarantor that a first-ranking had not been obtained. Moreover in the circumstances of this particular case the terms of the guarantee itself clearly excluded such a duty. Such cases of alleged misrepresentation by the lender will, of course, turn upon their own facts.[12]

[10] 1994 SLT (Sh Ct) 18

[11] 2003 SC 257

[12] Cf: *Royal Bank of Scotland plc -v- O'Donnell* 2015 SC 258, where the misrepresentation was considered sufficient to found an action for reduction.

More recently, in a case seeking the reduction of a disposition and minute of agreement granted by a mother to her daughter and son in law on grounds of undue influence, *Young* was cited as authority for the proposition that it is insufficient merely to plead that a party did not understand what she was signing.[13] The point was conceded by counsel for the pursuer that parties are generally bound by what they sign, even if they have not troubled to read it.

Indeed, it appears to be the case that where the bank have made what might be considered a misrepresentation to the principal debtor, the guarantor cannot rely upon that misrepresentation in order to avoid liability under the guarantee. An example of that is found in *Barr -v- Dunbar Assets plc*,[14] where the lender had issued a letter to the debtor stating that they would require a joint and several guarantee from the two members of the business. However, in fact an individual guarantee was signed by one of the members instead. Importantly, the letter explaining that a joint guarantee would be required was not addressed to the member. His attempt to reduce that guarantee on the ground of having been misled by the letter to the principal debtor was unsuccessful. On the other hand, where the lender makes a misrepresentation to the guarantor themselves that misrepresentation can found an action for reduction of the guarantee, even where the misrepresentation is innocent.[15]

It is clear, therefore, that *Young* remains good law and tends to operate in the lender's favour in most cases. As we shall now see, however, influences from outside of Scotland began to form through the 1990's

[13] *Wilson -v- Watkins* [2019] CSOH 44: "*As a matter of generality it may not be very extraordinary for an adult of ordinary intelligence and competence to sign binding legal documents without having read them or, if having read them, not having fully understood them, but as [counsel] conceded, in such circumstances an adult of ordinary competence will usually be held bound by what she has chosen to add her signature to as an indication of agreement*" (per Lord Brodie at para [35]).

[14] [2016] CSOH 44

[15] *Royal Bank of Scotland plc -v- O'Donnell* 2015 SC 258, although see also *Bank of Ireland -v- Morton*, discussed above.

which were to lead to a conscious change in the law of Scotland by the House of Lords in 1997. As a result, the principle in *Young* now has a very important caveat in circumstances where the guarantee in question is being granted by the principal debtor's spouse or another person in a close personal relationship with them and there is a risk of undue influence being brought to bear.

CHAPTER THREE

DEVELOPMENTS IN ENGLAND & WALES

Pre-existing law

The law of England appears to have run upon similar lines to the law of Scotland, at least insofar as the close relationship between debtor and guarantor is concerned, for many years. The approach is typified by *National Westminster Bank plc -v- Morgan,*[16] a judgment of the House of Lords.

In that case a husband and wife, who were in financial difficulties with an ailing business and their building society threatening repossession under their mortgage approached the plaintiff bank for a refinance. The bank agreed to a short-term advance of £14,500 subject to a legal charge over the house by both husband and wife. The couple already had a second legal charge over the property in favour of the bank, but that charge had been limited to £6,000. They were now being asked to grant an unlimited charge. The finance was negotiated by the husband and in due course the bank's manager attended at the house to obtain the wife's signature. The funds were transferred and the original mortgage repaid. The immediate threat of repossession was thereby averted.

The judgment describes the meeting at the house as follows:

> "[The bank agent's] conversation with Mrs. Morgan lasted only five minutes. Mrs. Morgan's concern was lest the document which she was being asked to sign might enable the husband to borrow from the bank for business purposes. She wanted the charge confined to paying off the Abbey National and to the provision of bridging finance for about five weeks. She told [the

[16] [1985] AC 686

> bank's agent] that she had no confidence in her husband's business ability and did not want the mortgage to cover his business liabilities. Mr. Barrow advised her that the cover was so limited."[17]

The husband was not present in the meeting, but "was in and out of the room, 'hovering around'. Mrs Morgan made it clear to [the bank] that she did not want him there"[18]. In her defence to the action raised by the bank following default, the wife argued that the bank had exerted undue influence over her in order to procure her signature. In fact, the Charge was unlimited and would not have prevented any further business borrowing by Mr Morgan from being secured by the Charge (albeit it does not appear that any such borrowing was sought or advanced).

It was found at first instance that both husband and wife had a high degree of anxiety over the prospect of losing their home and that that they knew that there was no other way of saving the house. It was found that the bank's manager had not pressured the wife to sign and that there was no duty on the bank in the circumstances to advise the wife to take independent legal advice. In those circumstances the judge at first instance held in the bank's favour. This was overturned by the Court of Appeal. The bank appealed to the House of Lords.

The House of Lords allowed the bank's appeal, holding that undue influence required the victimisation of one party by the other as well as a transaction which had been wrongful in the sense that it was either manifestly unfair or disadvantageous to the wronged party. Evidence of the relationship between the parties was not of itself sufficient to raise a presumption of undue influence. A party also required to show that the transaction was wrongful or had taken advantage of the person subject to the influence. In this case, the relationship between the bank and the wife

---

[17] *Ibid* at p.701 *per* Lord Scarman

[18] *Ibid.*

was a normal business relationship and the transaction had not been disadvantageous to the wife.

In the Court of Appeal it had been held that certain types of "confidential" relationship can give rise to a presumption of undue influence without the need for proof of a disadvantageous outcome. This conclusion was rejected by the House:

> "There are plenty of confidential relationships which do not give rise to the presumption of undue influence (a notable example is that of husband and wife, *Bank of Montreal v. Stuart* [1911] A.C. 120); and there are plenty of nonconfidential relationships in which one person relies upon the advice of another, e.g. many contracts for the sale of goods. Nor am I persuaded that the charge, limited as it was by Mr. Barrow's declaration to securing the loan to pay off the Abbey National debt and interest during the bridging period, was disadvantageous to Mrs. Morgan. It meant for her the rescue of her home upon the terms sought by her – a short-term loan at a commercial rate of interest."[19]

Morgan concerned a claim of undue influence of a bank over a borrower. However, the principle that the transaction must be shown to be disadvantageous to the wronged party had been held to apply even where actual undue influence by one spouse over another has been held to exist (unless the lender has actual or constructive knowledge of the undue influence).[20] Manifest disadvantage in this context required a balance between the risk and effect of enforcement against the guarantor on the one hand and the benefits gained by the transaction on the other.[21]

---

[19] *Ibid., per* Lord Scarman at p.703

[20] *Bank of Credit & Commerce International SA -v- Aboody* [1990] 1 QB 923

[21] See *Ibid.,* per Slade LJ at p.965 "*Whenever a guarantee or charge is given, there is always the risk that the guarantee may be called in or the charge enforced. Therefore, as Miss Williamson submitted, the question whether the assumption of such a risk is manifestly disadvantageous to the giver must depend on the balance of two factors, namely, (a) the seriousness of the risk of enforcement to the giver, in practical terms; and (b) the*

O'Brien

Such was the state of the law in 1993 when the House of Lords issued their judgment in *Barclays Bank plc -v- O'Brien.*[22]

The facts in *O'Brien* will become rather familiar as this book progresses due to their similarity to cases which followed. A husband and wife agreed to execute a second mortgage over their home in favour of the bank. The mortgage was to secure overdraft facilities to a company of which the husband was a shareholder, but not the wife. The wife had been told by her husband that the mortgage was limited to £60,000 and would last for three weeks. This was not true. The wife signed the deed without reading it in reliance on these statements, and also signed a side letter which stated *inter alia* that she has been advised by the bank to seek independent legal advice. In fact she had not been advised by the bank to seek independent legal advice, did not seek such advice, and nor had she read the side letter before signing.

The company's overdraft climbed to £154,000 and entered default. The bank sought to enforce the mortgage and obtained a judgement for possession. The wife appealed, which was refused on the grounds that there was no evidence that the husband acted as agent for the bank and the bank could not be found liable for his actions.

At the Court of Appeal the wife was successful. The Court identified that there were two strands of authority, one based on agency which would afford no protection to the wife in the circumstances of this case; the other based in equity which would provide protections to certain classes of surety based on the nature of the relationship between the debtor and surety. The court held that the wife was entitled to special protection in equity and that the mortgage was only enforceable to the extent of

benefits gained by the giver in accepting the risk. The judge, after a full and careful examination of the background to each of the six transactions, carried out this balancing exercise and came to the conclusion that as a matter of fact no manifest disadvantage had been shown."

22 [1994] 1 AC 180

£60,000 (which had been satisfied). The bank appealed to the House of Lords.

Before the Lords, the bank argued that if one took the Court of Appeal's reasoning to its limit, equity would provide a remedy to any married woman, even in the absence of any undue pressure, misrepresentation or impropriety by her husband and whether or not there was a disadvantage. This would apply merely on the grounds that she (a) was married and (b) had misunderstood the transaction. The bank argued that correct approach was to look at the effect of the principal debtor's undue influence, misrepresentation or other impropriety in a similar manner to the cases we have already examined. To give married women a different treatment from that afforded to other guarantors would be a regressive step "incompatible with the modern concepts of the status of women".[23]

Mrs O'Brien argued that equitable relief is available to parties involved in unfair transactions to protect them from dishonesty. The concepts of presumed undue influence (a rebuttable presumption) and unconscionable bargain had been developed with this aim in mind. "Equity has treated married women differently from, and more tenderly than, other third parties who provide security for the debts of others".[24]

Having heard argument, the Lords dismissed the bank's appeal.

In the lead judgment, Lord Browne-Wilkinson considered the policy considerations which faced the courts. This included changes to society which have resulted in higher proportions of wealth being invested in the family home, and the move towards equality of the sexes. Restrictions on women owning property had been removed and in modern times most homes are jointly owned between husband and wife. The homes also, generally, represent the largest matrimonial asset. As the main asset, the

[23] *Ibid.,* at p.184

[24] *Ibid.,* at p.185

family home is the natural source of security where a spouse wishes to raise finance for business purposes.

Whilst these changes had also led to a less patriarchal approach to the position of married women in society, "the practice does not yet coincide with the ideal"[25] and many wives remained subordinate to their husbands in financial affairs. Nevertheless:

> "...it is important to keep a sense of balance in approaching these cases. It is easy to allow sympathy for the wife who is threatened with the loss of her home at the suit of a rich bank to obscure an important public interest viz., the need to ensure that the wealth currently tied up in the matrimonial home does not become economically sterile. If the rights secured to wives by the law renders vulnerable loans granted on the security of matrimonial homes, institutions will be unwilling to accept such security, thereby reducing the flow of loan capital to business enterprises. It is therefore essential that a law designed to protect the vulnerable does not render the matrimonial home unacceptable as security to financial institutions."

Thus, having set the scene, the court went on to consider the law of undue influence and the development of the law in this area. It was demonstrated that whilst there was no automatic presumption of undue influence by a husband over a wife, the law had traditionally been more ready to find undue influence proven in a case involving husband and wife than in other cases. It was concluded that:

> "...this special tenderness of treatment afforded to wives by the courts is properly attributable to two factors. First, many cases may well fall into the Class ... of [presumed] undue influence because the wife demonstrates that she placed trust and confidence in her husband in relation to her financial affairs and therefore raises a presumption of undue influence. Second, the

[25] *Ibid.*, at p.188

> sexual and emotional ties between the parties provide a ready weapon for undue influence: a wife's true wishes can easily be overborne because of her fear of destroying or damaging the wider relationship between her and her husband if she opposes his wishes."[26]

However the court recognised that there was an additional element in this case – the involvement of the bank. The bank had not directly exercised undue influence over Mrs O'Brien and was not directly responsible for the actions of Mr O'Brien. A remedy might present itself if the husband were acting as agent for the bank, but otherwise no legal remedy arises.

Aside from this, if a creditor bank has actual or constructive notice of the undue influence exercised by the husband, this would put the bank on notice of the wife's right in equity to have the transaction set aside. If the transaction proceeded, the bank would therefore take the security subject to that equity and would be vulnerable to the transaction being set aside (albeit as a purchaser for value).

Having undertaken this analysis, the Lords rejected the reasoning of the Court of Appeal insofar as it sought to apply a special equity to wives engaged in surety transactions.[27] However, the court did consider that wives engaged in such transactions should be afforded additional protection by law and proceeded to identify a legal basis for it. That basis

---

[26] *Ibid.*, at p.190

[27] *Ibid.*, at p.195, *per* Lord Browne-Wilkinson: "*In my judgment, the special equity theory should be rejected. First, I can find no basis in principle for affording special protection to a limited class in relation to one type of transaction only. Second, to require the creditor to prove knowledge and understanding by the wife in all cases is to reintroduce by the back door either a presumption of undue influence … (which has been decisively rejected) or the* Romilly *heresy (which has long been treated as bad law). Third, although Scott L.J. found that there were two lines of cases one of which supported the special equity theory, on analysis although many decisions are not inconsistent with that theory the only two cases which support it are Yerkey v. Jones, 63 C.L.R. 649 , and the decision of the Court of Appeal in the present case.*"

was found in the doctrine of constructive notice. The lead judgment introduces the matter thus:

> "A wife who has been induced to stand as a surety for her husband's debts by his undue influence, misrepresentation or some other legal wrong has an equity as against him to set aside that transaction. Under the ordinary principles of equity, her right to set aside that transaction will be enforceable against third parties (e.g. against a creditor) if either the husband was acting as the third party's agent or the third party had actual or constructive notice of the facts giving rise to her equity. Although there may be cases where, without artificiality, it can properly be held that the husband was acting as the agent of the creditor in procuring the wife to stand as surety, such cases will be of very rare occurrence. The key to the problem is to identify the circumstances in which the creditor will be taken to have had notice of the wife's equity to set aside the transaction."[28]

The question in each case is whether there are facts known to the creditor which ought to have put him on inquiry as to the wife's rights to set aside the transaction. If there are, the creditor has constructive notice of the wife's rights and takes security subject to those rights.

Having earlier referred to the law's "tender treatment" of married women, the court then brought this concept to bear upon the general principle of constructive notice. The court concluded that because a wife is more likely to be subject to undue influence at the hands of her husband than other sureties, the mere fact of the parties being husband and wife is sufficient to put the bank on inquiry (unless there is a demonstrable advantage to the wife in the transaction). Once on inquiry in this way, the bank ought to take reasonable steps to satisfy themselves that the wife's agreement has been properly obtained failing which they will be deemed to have constructive notice of the wife's rights.

[28] *Ibid.* at p.195

Having established this principle, the lead judgment went on to consider what those reasonable steps ought to be:

> "It is plainly impossible to require of banks and other financial institutions that they should inquire of one spouse whether he or she has been unduly influenced or misled by the other. But in my judgment the creditor, in order to avoid being fixed with constructive notice, can reasonably be expected to take steps to bring home to the wife the risk she is running by standing as surety and to advise her to take independent advice....[F]or the future in my judgment a creditor will have satisfied these requirements if it insists that the wife attend a private meeting (in the absence of the husband) with a representative of the creditor at which she is told of the extent of her liability as surety, warned of the risk she is running and urged to take independent legal advice. If these steps are taken in my judgment the creditor will have taken such reasonable steps as are necessary to preclude a subsequent claim that it had constructive notice of the wife's rights"[29]

Additional steps may be required where the creditor has knowledge of further facts which make the existence of undue influence probable rather than possible. In those circumstances the creditor may be required to insist upon the wife being separately advised.

The court accepted that they "may" be extending the law in reaching this conclusion, but considered that this conclusion struck the required balance between protecting wives who rely implicitly upon their husband in relation to financial matters, and the need of financial institutions (and business) to lend upon the security of a family home. It was also noted that this judgment broadly accorded with accepted banking practice in relation to the taking of guarantees (aside from the need to ensure that the advice was given to the wife in a personal interview rather than in

[29] *Ibid.,* at p.196 *per* Lord Browne-Wilkinson

writing), and so did not impose an unreasonable burden upon financial institutions.

Finally, the court considered the question of whether the principle should extend beyond wives. It was concluded that it should:

> "The 'tenderness' shown by the law to married women is not based on the marriage ceremony but reflects the underlying risk of one cohabitee exploiting the emotional involvement and trust of the other. Now that unmarried cohabitation, whether heterosexual or homosexual, is widespread in our society, the law should recognise this. Legal wives are not the only group which are now exposed to the emotional pressure of cohabitation. Therefore if, but only if, the creditor is aware that the surety is cohabiting with the principal debtor, in my judgment the same principles should apply to them as apply to husband and wife."[30]

Likewise the principle might be applied to other relationships of trust and confidence, such as parent and child:

> "...in a case where the creditor is aware that the surety reposes trust and confidence in the principal debtor in relation to his financial affairs, the creditor is put on inquiry in just the same way as it is in relation to husband and wife."[31]

Thus the law of England & Wales was, if not extended, then at least innovated upon by the House of Lords in order to develop further protection to guarantors – primarily wives – who were cohabiting or in a close emotional relationship[32] with the principal debtor.[33] Following

[30] *Ibid.*, at p.198

[31] *Ibid.*

[32] See *Massey -v- Midland Bank plc* [1995] 1 All ER 929 – cohabitation is not an essential element of the test.

[33] Subsequent cases appear to have extended this principle even further, for example to employer/employee relationships: see *Credit Lyonnais Bank Nederland NV -v- Burch*

O'Brien, the House of Lords went on to hold that the principle applied even where monies were advanced to both husband and wife jointly, but the lender was aware that the monies would be applied for the husband's purposes rather than the couple's joint purposes.[34]

Etridge No. 2

After a few years, the House returned to the *O'Brien* principle and built upon it. *Royal Bank of Scotland plc -v- Etridge (No.2)*[35] was in fact eight conjoined appeals involving numerous lenders and parties. The common thread was lending to a business connected to one spouse and the giving of surety by the other. Seven of the cases involved a wife defending a claim for possession of the matrimonial home by the lender, the eighth was a claim by a wife for damages against her solicitor in relation to the advice she had received prior to entering the guarantee.

Under the *O'Brien* principle there was little doubt that the lenders were on inquiry. The question which the court sought to address in this case is what advice the wife requires to receive, and how independent must it be. As it was put by Lord Bingham of Cornhill:

> "The law must afford both parties [i.e. both the lender and the surety] a measure of protection. It cannot prescribe a code which will be proof against error, misunderstanding or mishap. But it can indicate minimum requirements which, if met, will reduce the risk of error, misunderstanding or mishap to an acceptable level. The paramount need in this important field is that these

[1997] 1 All ER 144. Effectively any relationship in which trust and confidence is reposed by the surety in the principal debtor is at risk for the lender.

34 *CIBC Mortgages plc -v- Pitt* [1994] 1 AC 200

35 [2002] 2 AC 773

> minimum requirements should be clear, simple and practically operable"[36]

The starting point was with the law of undue influence itself. Whilst the burden of proving undue influence in cases of husband and wife still rested with the surety, it was not an especially high bar. Proof that the surety placed trust and confidence in the other party in relation to the management of their financial affairs, coupled with a transaction which calls for explanation, will normally be sufficient to discharge the burden of proof and create a rebuttable presumption of undue influence.

When considering whether the presumption may be rebutted, the court may look at the advice which was received by the surety, but this may not be determinative of the issue.

> "The weight, or importance, to be attached to such advice depends on all the circumstances. In the normal course, advice from a solicitor or other outside adviser can be expected to bring home to a complainant a proper understanding of what he or she is about to do. But a person may understand fully the implications of a proposed transaction, for instance, a substantial gift, and yet still be acting under the undue influence of another. Proof of outside advice does not, of itself, necessarily show that the subsequent completion of the transaction was free from the exercise of undue influence"[37]

What was therefore required was some assurance that, whether or not advice had been given, undue influence was not a factor in the decision to proceed.

The House recognised that an attempt to meet this challenge had been made in *O'Brien*, but that it did not achieve its objective.[38] The Court

---

[36] *Ibid.*, at p.793

[37] *Ibid.*, at p.798 *per* Lord Nicholls of Birkenhead

[38] *Ibid.*, at p.801 *per* Lord Nicholls of Birkenhead: *"The House produced a practical solution. The House decided what are the steps a bank should take to ensure it is not*

also recognised that there were difficult cases. There may, for example, be a blurring of the lines where a wife becomes surety for the debts of a company in which she has a shareholding, although in such cases the court considered the principle is still activated as the holding of shares (or even directorships) do not necessarily equate to having conduct of the company's business.[39]

Banking practice had also not evolved in line with *O'Brien*. Banking practice remained that lenders did not generally have private meetings with wives as they did not wish to assume responsibility for any advice given in those meetings, and wished to avoid claims that undocumented things were said in those meetings which might be prejudicial to the bank's position.[40] Instead it had become almost standard practice for lenders to require wives to seek legal advice and to obtain written confirmation from the solicitor that they have explained the nature and effect of the document to the wife. This practice had not been the intention of *O'Brien* save in exceptional cases. An issue arising from the practice was the variance in quality of the legal advice being received. In many cases the advice was said to be perfunctory and to provide little or no protection to a wife contemplating such a transaction.

Having examined the difficulties which had arisen since *O'Brien*, the court turned to the question of what a lender should actually do to protect themselves. The answer to that question began with an examination of the duties of an independent solicitor advising the proposed surety. Those duties will be shaped by the solicitor's retainer and the circumstances of the case, but can broadly be summarised as follows[41]:-

---

affected by any claim the wife may have that her signature of the documents was procured by the undue influence or other wrong of her husband. Like every compromise, the outcome falls short of achieving in full the objectives of either of the two competing interests."

[39] *Ibid.*, at p.804

[40] *Ibid.*, at p. 804

[41] *Ibid.*, at p.807 *et seq.*

- The solicitor should explain the purpose of their involvement, and in particular that the lender will point to their involvement in meeting any argument that the wife was subject to undue influence or did not understand the transaction.

- The solicitor must explain the nature of the documents and the practical consequences these will have for the wife, including the potential to lose her home or be declared bankrupt.

- The seriousness of the risks must be pointed out and the wife informed of the purpose of the lending, the amount and principal terms of the facility (and of her guarantee) and that the bank may increase the facility or change its terms in the future without reference to her.

- The wife's financial means and assets should be explored, as should her understanding of the market value of the property which will be charged as part of the surety.

- The solicitor must state clearly that the wife has a choice, and that the decision to enter the transaction is hers alone. This may involve some further discussion of the present financial position and the couple's current exposure.

- The solicitor must then check whether the wife wishes to proceed and gain her consent to write to the bank confirming that he or she has explained the nature and practical implications of the documents.

- The meeting between solicitor and wife must be face to face and without the husband being present. Non-technical language must be used and the solicitor must obtain from the bank all of the information which they need.

- Whilst the advice must be independent, the court did not go so far as to bar the solicitor from acting on behalf of the husband, accepting that a solicitor advising the wife will have duties to her alone, and must be trusted to fulfil their professional ethical duties.

Having set out in detail the advice which a solicitor is expected to give to his client, the court then turned to the question of what would happen where the advice is wrong. In particular, what is the position of the bank who will have placed reliance upon the advice?

The conclusion reached by the court was that such cases are a matter between the wife and her solicitor. The bank should be able to rely on the fact of advice having been given in accordance with these guidelines, unless it knows or ought to know that the advice was not given or was defective.[42]

The next question is what steps the bank must take both before and upon receiving confirmation from the solicitor that the advice was given. Again, the court set out in prescriptive terms the steps which the lender must take[43]:

- The bank must check directly with the wife the name of the solicitor whom she wishes to act on her behalf and confirm that they will require written confirmation of the advice given for their own protection. An explanation of the reasons for that should be given and the wife should be told she may use the same solicitor as her husband if she wishes. The bank may not proceed unless it receives an appropriate response directly from the wife.

- The bank must provide all necessary financial information to the solicitor to enable the advice to be given.

---

42 *Ibid.*, p.811

43 *Ibid.*, at p. 811 *et seq.* See also the opinion of Lord Scott of Foscote at p.849 *et seq.*

- If the bank believes or suspects that the wife is not entering the transaction of her own free will, they must inform the solicitor of the facts giving rise to this suspicion.

- The bank must receive the written confirmation from the solicitor before proceeding.

- Nothing in any of the foregoing should prevent a bank official from giving the relevant advice to the wife if they wish to do so instead of a solicitor (i.e., the original solution proposed in *O'Brien* still stood and would still be effective).

Conclusion

The position in England and Wales, therefore, is a prescriptive one. Both lenders and solicitors giving advice to spouses have a list of minimum standards for how they must act. A heavy burden lies upon the solicitor who gives the independent advice, but equally the degree to which the bank is required to oversee the giving of the advice and provide information to the proposed guarantor represents a major departure from what was considered to be the pre-existing law.

In the meantime, the law of Scotland remained governed by the principle in *Young*. Given the shake-up of the law of England, however, it was probably only a matter of time before Scots law followed suit. All that would be required was a suitable case and a similar mindset in the House of Lords.

CHAPTER FOUR

SMITH -V- BANK OF SCOTLAND

Mr Smith and Mr Mumford were partners in a business called Kestrel Mirrored Wardrobes. In 1986 their business required funding and they approached the Bank of Scotland. The bank agreed to advance funding to them, but on condition that each of them granted security for the lending. Mr Smith owned his property jointly with his wife, and so Mrs Smith required to become a party to the transaction. Mr Mumford owned his home in his sole name. His wife did not require to be a party to the transaction, but she did require to give consent to it under the Matrimonial Homes (Family Protection)(Scotland) Act 1981 due to her occupancy rights under that statute. Neither wife had any direct interest in the business.

The effect of the transaction, in reality, was to have the wives act as cautioners for their husbands' business debts.

As is familiar in such cases, it was said that the wives had been misled by their husbands as to the nature and effect of the documents which they had signed. Neither wife took independent legal advice and nor did either of them receive a warning from the bank as to the potential consequences of signing the documents. The bank, as a matter of fact, had no knowledge of (nor took any interest in) the discussions which took place between husband and wife.

Emboldened by what was then the recent decision of *O'Brien* the wives raised proceedings within the Court of Session seeking partial reduction of the standard securities on the grounds of their husbands' allegedly fraudulent misrepresentations. Using the *O'Brien* ratio, it was argued that where the relationship between co-cautioners was a close one, such as husband and wife and it was clear that one party had no direct financial interest in the transaction, the lender should be deemed to be on inquiry and must satisfy themselves that the guarantor's consent had been properly obtained.

O'Brien, of course, was an English decision based on the law of England and Wales. It touched upon principles of the English legal system (such as equity) which are very different from Scots law. The law of Scotland, as we have already seen, was that set out in *Young -v- Clydesdale Bank* and *Royal Bank of Scotland -v- Greenshields.*[44] It was perhaps predictable, therefore, that Mrs Smith and Mrs Mumford were unsuccessful at First Instance[45]. It was held that in the absence of agency, or of actual knowledge of the husbands' misrepresentations, or of misrepresentation on the part of the bank itself, the bank had no duty to explain the nature or consequences of the transaction they were entering into.

> "What O'Brien seems to achieve is a presumption in favour of the wife of a wrong having been committed by the husband against her, created in the appropriate circumstances, particularly where there is no financial gain to her in relation to the debts being guaranteed and the actual transaction is to her financial disadvantage. I am not prepared against the background of the long-established Scots authorities referred to by counsel for the defenders with regard to the duty, or lack of it, owed by a bank to the cautioner, to import such a presumption into the law of Scotland"[46]

On appeal to the Inner House[47], the first instance decision was upheld. The Division held that there was no presumption of undue influence known to the law of Scotland, and that the claim could only proceed if the bank had knowledge of facts and circumstances tending to show that undue influence was being exercised. All that the averments in this case suggested was that the bank knew of the relationship of husband and wife

---

[44] See Chapter 2

[45] 1994 SC 613

[46] *Ibid.*, at p. 618 per Lord Johnston

[47] 1996 SLT 392

and that the transaction was not to the financial advantage of the wives, but that the bank made no further inquiries. That was not sufficient.

In the judgment, the court pointed to a fundamental difference between the law of Scotland and the law of England in relation to undue influence:

> "In our opinion the tendency in English law to deal with cases of undue influence by reference to presumptions arising from the fact that the parties are related to each other differs significantly from the approach to cases of undue influence in Scots law. *Walker, Civil Remedies (1974), p 155* states that, while in England a presumption of undue influence arises in certain relationships which may be rebutted, in Scots law there is never a presumption."[48]

As the presumption of undue influence lies at the heart of *O'Brien*, it could not be said to form part of the law of Scotland and the pursuers' case must therefore fail. Moreover, whilst better explanations by lenders might be desirable, extension of the law by the judiciary was considered by the court to be undesirable:

> "We are unable to find any sound basis in Scots law for such a wide extension of the duties of the creditor beyond those which have been so clearly stated in the Scottish authorities. If these duties are thought to be in need of extension, it would be preferable that this should be done by the legislature after detailed consideration of all the issues by the Scottish Law Commission."[49]

Thus the case arrived where it seems it was always destined to go – before the House of Lords.[50] Notably it was only Mrs Smith who took the case

[48] *Ibid.,* at p.397

[49] *Ibid.* at p.398

[50] 1997 SC (HL) 111

to the Lords, Mrs Mumford having dropped out after the appeal to the Inner House. Whilst there was no dissenting judgment as such, it would be wrong to say that the decision of the House was made without trepidation on the part of at least one member of the panel:

> "My Lords, while I can follow the policy reasons for clothing a creditor with constructive knowledge of the risk of undue influence by a husband in the special circumstances of a cautionary obligation I have the greatest difficulty in seeing why such constructive knowledge should extend to misrepresentation. There has so far as I am aware never been any suggestion in the law of Scotland that any particular class of persons is more likely to misrepresent in relation to a contract than any other class. Applying the principles of Scots law alone I would therefore have been disposed to dismiss this appeal. Nevertheless I am conscious that your Lordships do not share my difficulties and I appreciate the practical advantages of applying the same law to identical transactions in both jurisdictions"[51]

Some disquiet notwithstanding, therefore, the House allowed the appeal.

Lord Clyde delivered the lead judgment, and began by setting the scene:

> "The case proceeds on the basis of fact that the bank manager knew that the grant of the standard security was over a dwellinghouse which was the matrimonial home of the pursuer and her husband, that the grant was not to the financial advantage of the pursuer, that it was in security of the pursuer's husband's business debts and that the pursuer had no involvement nor interest in that business. The pursuer and her husband signed the security documents at the office of the bank's solicitors, but she was given no opportunity of perusing the

[51] *Ibid.*, per Lord Jauncey at p. 115

> document, was not given a copy of it and was not given nor advised to obtain any independent advice."[52]

Lord Clyde went on to explain the nature of the husband's misrepresentation and to identify the general rule applying to such cases under the law of Scotland. That general rule was the one identified in *Young*, namely that a misrepresentation by a third party does not invalidate a voluntary obligation. That rule applies in both cases of misrepresentation and in cases of undue influence. It is, however, subject to an important further principle in cases where fraud is involved:

> "The principle here, as formulated in *Schofield v. Templer* and quoted by Lord Shand in *Clydesdale Bank v. Paul* at pp 628–629 is: 'a person cannot avail himself of what has been obtained by the fraud of another, unless he is not only innocent of the fraud but has given some valuable consideration.'."[53]

Lord Clyde also identified further exceptions in relation to facility and circumvention and extortion, particularly where the contract is void for want of consent rather than voidable.

Having found that there was no general duty upon a creditor to disclose to the guarantor the financial position of the debtor, Lord Clyde then identified exceptions to that general rule. Those exceptions were:

- where the lender reasonably believes fraud to have been involved in the gaining of consent, they must make inquiry; and

- where the lender makes a representation to the cautioner, either spontaneously or in answer to a question, they must be full and fair in that representation.

---

[52] *Ibid.,* at p.116

[53] *Ibid.,* at p.117

The court identified both of these exceptions as being underpinned by the concept of good faith.

Finally, Lord Clyde reached the nub of the matter:

> "In *O'Brien* this House consciously sought to extend the law of England. The question for your Lordships is whether a corresponding extension should be made to the law of Scotland."[54]

The Court recognised that the laws of Scotland and England prior to *O'Brien* had been broadly the same. Moreover the House considered the policy considerations underpinning *O'Brien* were equally applicable to Scotland. The only difference which the House had been pointed to between the two jurisdictions was the law of undue influence, in that the law of Scotland was said not to recognise any presumptions of undue influence in the same manner as appears to be accepted in England. The "invalidating tendency" or "tender treatment of wives" could not be readily identified as being part of the law of Scotland as it had been in England.

Having considered the representations made by Counsel for the bank on the dangers of imposing uniformity across both jurisdictions, Lord Clyde concluded that the extension of the law to Scotland might in fact be advantageous: "when similar transactions with similar institutions or indeed branches of the same institutions may be taking place in both countries there is a clear practical advantage in the preservation of corresponding legal provisions".[55]

Having determined that the extension of the *O'Brien* principle to Scotland was desirable, the question then became one of how this might be achieved without offending the Scottish legal system. The law of England, particularly in relation to the operation of equity, is markedly

[54] *Ibid.,* at p. 118

[55] *Ibid.,* at p.120

different from the law of Scotland notwithstanding that similar outcomes are often achieved in each. A means was therefore required to transpose the *O'Brien* principle into Scots law without using English legal concepts.

The House considered whether the concept of "constructive notice" might afford a solution. Under this remedy, the bank would be taken to have notice of a fraud through their knowledge of facts and circumstances (i.e. the close relationship of husband and wife) which put them on inquiry. There was some authority for that concept being part of the law of Scotland, albeit applying it to Mrs Smith's case was recognised as potentially being a stretch. The court therefore elected not to fix the creditor with constructive notice of wrongdoing.

Lord Clyde's preference was instead to pin the principle on the concept of good faith.[56] It had already been shown that the lack of a duty on the part of a creditor to give advice to a guarantor was subject to exceptions. It was therefore a simple matter to extend this to situations where the lender "should reasonably suspect that there may be factors bearing on the participation of the cautioner which might undermine the validity of the contract through his or her intimate relationship with the debtor".[57]

Lord Clyde was clear that this extension did not require any additional duty of investigation, but that it would require the lender to be deemed a potential participant in any misrepresentation of the debtor. Moreover the duty would only arise:

> "...if the circumstances of the case are such as to lead a reasonable man to believe that owing to the personal relationship between the debtor and the proposed cautioner the latter's consent may not be fully informed or freely given. Of course if the creditor, acting honestly and in good faith, has no reason to believe that

---

56 *Ibid.*, at p.121: " ...*it seems to me preferable to recognise the element of good faith which is required of the creditor on the constitution of a contract of cautionary and find there a proper basis for decision.*"

57 *Ibid.*

> there is any particularly close relationship between the debtor and the proposed cautioner the duty will not arise."[58]

This left only the question of how a lender would comply with this new duty. We have seen that the initial *O'Brien* case intended the process to be relatively light touch. Lord Clyde maintained that approach here.

- In the first place, it was not for the creditor to investigate whether there was, in fact, conduct which vitiated the contract. All the creditor requires to do is "maintain good faith".
- Maintaining good faith in this context would require a creditor to:
    - warn the guarantor of the consequences of entering into the proposed cautionary obligations; and
    - advise him or her to take independent advice.[59]

The creditors other rights and duties remained as before. As had been recognised by the Inner House before them, the House identified that the Code of Practice adopted by most major banks and building societies at the time contained broadly similar duties. It was commented that compliance with the Code might therefore lessen any practical impact of this ruling.

Consequently, as they had in England & Wales, the House of Lords effected a conscious extension of the law of Scotland to offer additional protection to (primarily) wives entering into cautionary arrangements in relation to their husbands' businesses. It is fair to say that the reaction of the profession and academics in Scotland was not universally welcoming

---

[58] *Ibid.*

[59] *Ibid.*, p.122

of this development.[60] The issue now was whether the law of Scotland would develop in lockstep with the law of England, including adopting the very prescriptive approach seen in *Etridge*.

Subsequent cases would now be vital in seeking to shape this new law.

---

[60] See, *e.g.*, G L Gretton, "Sexually Transmitted Debt", 1997 SLT (News) 195. Although coverage was not universally negative: see, e.g., D Pope, "Scots law takes actual notice of Barclays Bank -v- O'Brien", 1997 12(12) JIBL 493

CHAPTER FIVE

DEVELOPMENT OF THE LAW POST-SMITH

As with any change to the established law, a significant amount of testing of the boundaries was about to occur. The late 1990's and early 2000's became, for those involved in banking litigation, the era of the "Smith-Type" case. The relative brevity of Lord Clyde's dicta and the extensive development of the law in England beyond the original *O'Brien* principle meant there was a lot to test, and a fertile period in Scottish litigation ensued.

Was *Smith* retrospective?

Perhaps the most important question to arise from *Smith* was whether the ruling which Lord Clyde had made was retrospective. The House had stated in terms that the ruling was an "extension" of the law, and so it was a logical question as to whether that extension was retrospective or only applies to cases or lending post-Smith. If the latter, what date would this run from?

The practical importance of this was obvious – a lender's understanding of the concept of good faith prior to *Smith*, would be very different from their understanding post-*Smith*. Lenders will have been entering into transactions for a number of years believing themselves to have been in compliance with their duties. Could those transactions now be unpicked?

Generally speaking, judge made law is retrospective in nature. Initial academic opinion strongly suggested that the law was indeed retrospective, and that this would call into question every cautionary obligation entered into by a wife before or since.[61]

The point was first judicially considered in *Clydesdale Bank plc -v- Black.*[62] In that case the lender had sought to enforce their standard security over the defender's home which secured *inter alia* business lending. Within the Sheriff Court at first instance, decree had been granted. The defender's appeal to the Sheriff Principal was refused and so an appeal was taken to the Court of Session.

The calling up notice referenced a sum of £50,000 which was due under a personal guarantee by the defender. That personal guarantee related to the defender's husband's business, DEM1 Limited. The guarantee was regulated by the Consumer Credit Act, and so contained statutory wording which included a warning that "You may have to pay instead of the debtor" and that "you should take independent legal advice before signing this guarantee". Whilst the standard security does not appear to have contained such a warning, it was admitted that the defender had independent legal advice in relation to the standard security which collateralised the guarantee. Notwithstanding these facts, the defender put forward a defence based on *Smith* and also sought to argue that the *Etridge (No.2)* principles should be extended to Scotland, meaning the content of the solicitors' advice should have been more closely managed by the lender.

[61] See, e.g., G.L. Gretton, "Sexually Transmitted Debt", 1997 SLT (News) 195 at p. 197 "Moreover, the new law is retrospective. That is one of the problems about judicial legislation. Whereas Parliamentary legislation is prospective only, and does not (in general) affect earlier events, judicial legislation is both prospective and retrospective, for, by a fiction, it is deemed always to have been the law. There will now be numerous cautionary obligations which, when entered into, were valid, but which are now retrospectively made voidable at the instance of the cautioner."

[62] 2002 SC 555

In the course of their judgments, the judges each considered the question of whether the principle in *Smith* should be retrospective. Lord Coulsfield sets out the issue thus:

> "What the pursuers did in this case complied exactly with the requirements of good faith and proper banking practice, as understood in Scotland at the time. The distinction between the tests to be applied to past actings and future actings is clearly recognised in the cases. It is true, as Lord Marnoch points out, that normally a court decision on a question of common law is regarded as stating the law as it always has been. In this case, however, we are dealing with the effects of decisions which expressly extended the law and expressly distinguished between consequences for past transactions and consequences for future transactions."[63]

Lord Marnoch, in his judgment, rejected the suggestion that the judgment in Smith should be anything other than retrospective in its effect:

> "Court decisions which affect the common law are of their nature retrospective in character, even if they touch on what appear to be subjective matters such as the presence or absence of good faith. In such cases the real question remains what, in the eyes of the law at its present stage of development, is treated as satisfying the requirement in question. The passage from the speech of Lord Nicholls of Birkenhead which is quoted above was, for example, both recognised and intended to have retrospective effect although there are, of course, other passages in both *O'Brien* and *Etridge (No 2)* which, rather unusually, bear to relate only to the future. In any event, I am satisfied that the submission in question should in general be rejected."[64]

---

63 *Ibid.,* at p.566

64 *Ibid.,* at p.569

Lords Sutherland and Coulsfield disagreed, however, and opined that the law as expounded in *Smith* was not intended to be retrospective in nature. Lord Sutherland put the point as follows:-

> "At these times the law relating to the issue was set out by the Inner House decision in *Smith*. Even though the appeal to the House of Lords was allowed, that was done on the basis of a 'development' in the law of Scotland to recognise the decision in *O'Brien* and to ensure conformity of approach in both jurisdictions. In my opinion, in considering what was the appropriate duty owed by a creditor in November 1996, the law to be looked at is that contained in the Inner House decision in *Smith*, particularly as the issue involves whether or not the creditor was acting in good faith. It seems to me that it would be difficult to say that someone was not acting in good faith when he was complying directly with the law apparently in force at that time."

Hence it appears that *Smith* is not retrospective and that in considering the duties incumbent upon a lender prior to *Smith* it is the Inner House's judgment in *Smith* that must be looked to (which in turn upheld the principles in *Young*, which were examined above). It is perhaps worth noting that in addition to the academic opinion to the contrary, there is some Sheriff Court authority which pre-dates *Black* where the security dated from 1972, and a proof was allowed.[65] Nevertheless, in light of the opinion of the majority of the Inner House in *Black* such authority should be treated with caution.

Is an actionable wrong required before *Smith* can be applied?

A further issue to arise from *Smith* was what would happen where the bank breached the duty set out in that case, but there had in fact been no

[65] *Royal Bank of Scotland plc -v- Clark* 2000 SLT (Sh Ct) 101

undue influence or misrepresentation of any kind by the husband. Could the bank lose their security merely by failing to give the relevant warning?

This point was considered in *Braithwaite -v- Bank of Scotland.*[66] In this case, a wife pledged a portfolio of shares and unit trusts to a Bank which was intended as security for debts due by her husband's business. An action was subsequently raised by her seeking a declarator that the bank had no right to intromit with the shares and unit trusts and for reduction of the letter of pledge.

One strand of her case related to the *Smith* ratio. It was argued for Mrs Braithwaite that the Bank knew that she was co-habiting with her husband, but had failed to give her a warning as to the nature and consequences of the obligation to which she was entering. It was averred that she was told "very little" about her husband's business affairs. It was further averred that the bank

> "...was aware that the pursuer relied on her husband in relation to their financial affairs. The pursuer was frightened of him. He is a man of vicious and, on occasion, violent temper. He regularly presented documents to the pursuer for her signature on a variety of pretexts. If the pursuer questioned their contents, he became infuriated. Accordingly, she did not dare refuse to sign."[67]

Further averments stated that she had been presented only with the last page of the document, and had been told that it would authorise the bank to sell shares "as required for the purpose of management of her portfolio".

It was argued on Mrs Braithwaite's behalf that no averments of wrongdoing were required, and that is was sufficient that the bank had failed to advise or warn Mrs Braithwaite of the consequences of the transaction. Mrs Braithwaite was unsuccessful on this point. The Lord

[66] 1999 SLT 25

[67] *Ibid.,* at p.31

Ordinary held that proof of an actionable wrong would be required in order for a financial institution to be deprived of their security. This was the logical result of *Smith*:

> "The basis on which that institution could not enforce the security against the wife was that it had constructive notice of the wrong which had been perpetrated against her. It could not have such notice unless such a wrong had in fact been perpetrated. It would be remarkable if the effect of *Smith v Bank of Scotland* on Scots law was to dispense with the need for a pursuer to prove a similar wrong perpetrated in fact by her husband."[68]

Accordingly, it appears that a failure by a lender to comply with the duty set out in *Smith* might yet be saved if there was in fact no wrongdoing on the part of the husband. Unlike the law of England, there is no presumption of undue influence under the law of Scotland upon which a spouse can rely.

How independent does the advice require to be?

As we have seen, the English courts in *Etridge (No.2)* saw no issue with a solicitor acting for both debtor and guarantor. The House considered that a lender ought to be able to rely upon the professionalism of the solicitor to keep himself or herself free of conflict.

A similar point was considered in Scotland in the case of *Forsyth -v- Royal Bank of Scotland plc.*[69] In that case Mrs Forsyth and her husband granted a standard security in favour of the bank over their matrimonial home. That security related to Mr Forsyth's business, and it was averred that Mr Forsyth had told his wife that the security did not put her home at risk

---

[68] *Ibid.*, at p.33

[69] 2000 SLT 1295

and that she had accepted that representation. She stated that she would not have signed the security but for that representation.

In due course Mrs Forsyth raised an action for reduction of the standard security, and the question arose as to what advice she had received from the bank. The bank averred that a firm of solicitors had acted on behalf of all three parties to the action, and that the bank remained in good faith in circumstances where the bank reasonably believed that advice was being given to the pursuer on the import of the documents being signed.

Mrs Forsyth admitted that the solicitors acted for her husband and for the bank, but denied that she had given them any instructions to act for her. At debate it was conceded on her behalf that the relevant issue was not whether she had given her instructions to the solicitor, but whether the bank reasonably believed that she had. The point at issue for the pursuer was therefore whether the bank was entitled to assume that she had been given the advice which *Smith* requires of a lender in circumstances where the solicitor in question acts for more than one party to the transaction?

In his judgment the Lord Ordinary concluded that:

> "In my opinion the creditor is ordinarily entitled to assume that the solicitor will have acted in accordance with his professional obligations towards his client. The possibility exists, of course, that a solicitor will fail to fulfil his professional obligations. But if he does so fail, the client will ordinarily have recourse against him for any loss which she suffers as a result. It would, in my view, be going too far to say that good faith requires that the creditor make the assumption that the solicitor may fail to fulfil his professional duties. The position would, of course, be different if the creditor were aware of circumstances that

> indicated that the solicitor had not fulfilled, or would not fulfil, his professional duties to his client."[70]

The "circumstances" referred to in this passage and which the creditor requires to be aware of must go beyond mere knowledge that the solicitor is acting for more than one party. It is for the solicitor to reconcile his or her duties to their various clients and to act in accordance with their duties:

> "The mere fact that the solicitor is acting for more than one party in the transaction is not, in my view, sufficient to displace the creditor's entitlement to assume that the solicitor will, in his capacity as the solicitor to the granter of the security, fulfil his professional obligation to advise her about the nature and consequences of the transaction. It seems to me that part of the assumption that the solicitor will act properly is that he will pay due regard to the rules of professional conduct in relation to conflicts of interest."[71]

The Lord Ordinary took comfort from the fact that this conclusion accorded with the conclusions reached by the House of Lords in *Etridge (No.2)*, notwithstanding that case arose from and was governed by the law of England.

It is important to note, however, that the lender must have a reasonable belief that the guarantor is or has obtained legal advice in relation to the transaction. If they do not have such a belief, there is no protection for the lender. In *Broadway -v- Clydesdale Bank plc (No.1)*[72] a lender sought dismissal of a claim for reduction of a standard security on the grounds that the pursuer had been legally advised. However the court refused to grant the motion as the correspondence did not contain an unequivocal inference that the solicitors were acting for the pursuer. In those

---

[70] *Ibid.*, at p.1304

[71] *Ibid.*

[72] 2000 GWD 19-763

circumstances the lender must make further inquiries to ensure that advice is being taken.[73]

What is the substance of the advice which the lender requires to give?

Clydesdale Bank plc –v- Black[74], has been mentioned above. It was another case in which a wife, having taken independent legal advice, granted a security and personal guarantee to the bank in relation to her husband's business borrowings.

The bank raised proceedings seeking to enforce the security in the Sheriff court. The defender contended that she had signed the deed without being aware of its true nature and under the undue influence of her husband. At first instance the Sheriff granted decree *de plano*. On appeal to the Sheriff Principal, the Sheriff's decision was affirmed. Mrs Black then appealed to the Inner House.

It was averred that Mrs Black had signed the guarantee without being aware of its import. That she reposed trust and confidence in her husband in relation to financial matters, and that he concealed the nature of the document from her. She admitted having obtained independent legal advice, but did not disclose the content of that advice.

[73] It is worth noting that in *Broadway -v- Clydesdale Bank plc (No.2)* 2003 SLT 707, the court considered the question anew: "In *Smith* there was no suggestion that the pursuer had the benefit of legal advice when entering into the transaction, and the steps which Lord Clyde identified as being necessary to preserve the lender's good faith must be seen in that context. In a number of subsequent cases it has been held that if the lender knows or has reasonable cause to believe that the granter of the standard security has the benefit of legal advice in connection with the transaction, good faith does not require the lender to give the warning and advice contemplated in Smith (see Forsyth , Wright and Etridge (No 2)). In such circumstances the lender's good faith is adequately evidenced by his entering into the transaction in the knowledge or reasonable belief that the granter of the security has the benefit of legal advice." (at p.725) It was found that Mrs Broadway had indeed had legal advice.

[74] 2002 SC 555

The guarantee in question contained wording which, had it been read, would have provided warning of the import of the document and advised the guarantor to take advice:

> "The guarantee bore to be given in respect of the obligations of James Black under a loan account, the initial amount of which was stated as £150,000, but contained a provision that the grantor's liability was limited to £50,000 plus interest. The conditions of the guarantee, which are lengthy, are set out in twenty three clauses. On the last page of the document, after the final numbered clause which deals with governing law, the document contains the following passage: 'IMPORTANT – YOU SHOULD READ THIS CAREFULLY. YOUR RIGHTS The Consumer Credit Act 1974 covers this guarantee and indemnity and lays down certain requirements for your protection. If they are not carried out the bank cannot enforce the guarantee and indemnity against you without a court order. Until the agreement between the bank and the debtor has been made, you can change your mind about giving the guarantee and indemnity. If you wish to withdraw, you must give WRITTEN notice to the bank which must reach it BEFORE the main agreement is made. Once it has been made you can no longer change your mind. Under this guarantee and indemnity YOU MAY HAVE TO PAY INSTEAD of the debtor and fulfil any other obligations under the guarantee and indemnity. (But you cannot be made to pay more than he could have been made to pay unless he is under 18.) However, if the debtor fails to keep to his side of the agreement the bank must send him a default notice (and a copy to you) giving him a chance to put things right before any claim is made on you. If you would like to know more about your rights under the Act you should contact either your local Trading Standards Department or your nearest Citizen's Advice Bureau. You should take independent legal advice before signing this guarantee and indemnity. The maximum which you may be required to pay is limited to the sums referred to at the beginning of this document. ACKNOWLEDGEMENT I/we acknowledge

> that, when this guarantee was presented or sent for the purpose of being signed by or on behalf of me/us there was also presented or sent one copy of this guarantee each for me/us to keep.'
>
> There is then a section, which is given emphasis by being enclosed in a box, which contains the following words: 'This is a guarantee and indemnity subject to the Consumer Credit Act 1974. If the debtor fails to keep to his agreement with the bank YOU MAY HAVE TO PAY INSTEAD and fulfil any other obligations under the guarantee and indemnity. Sign only if you want to be legally bound by its terms.'"75

That wording was vital in the result. As Lord Marnoch went on to point out[76]:

> "… these legends complied, almost to the letter, with para 12.1 of the Code of Banking Practice adopted by banks and building societies in Scotland in March 1992. What is more, I am of opinion that they comply exactly with what was desiderated by Lord Clyde in the passage in *Smith* cited above. After referring to the taking of 'reasonable steps' Lord Clyde goes on to say that: 'So far as the substance of those steps is concerned it seems to me that it would be sufficient for the creditor to warn the potential cautioner of the consequences of entering into the proposed cautionary obligation and to advise him or her to take independent advice'. He then goes on to approve, in terms, of the Code of Practice referred to above saying only that it 'might extend more widely than is required by the duty which I have described in so far as it may not be limited to cases where a close personal relationship exists…'. I accordingly demur to the suggestion advanced by counsel for the defender and appellant that Lord Clyde, and those of their Lordships who agreed with Lord Clyde, in some way imported into Scots law the more

[75] *Ibid.,* at p.556 *per* Lord Coulsfield

[76] *Ibid.,* at p.568

> precise requirements previously set out for England by Lord Browne-Wilkinson in Barclays Bank plc v O'Brien."

What can be taken from this case, therefore, is that the more prescriptive approach of English law has been rejected by the Inner House, and that a warning in writing within the body of the deed is sufficient in most cases to maintain the good faith which a lender is required to demonstrate.

At what stage is "good faith" measured?

As we have seen, the requirement arising out of Smith is that a lender must maintain good faith by giving the spouse a warning as to the consequences of the transaction and advising the spouse to take independent legal advice. We have also seen that these steps can be avoided if the lender reasonably believes that the spouse is receiving independent advice. A question may arise, however, as to whether the lender has an ongoing duty to advise where the nature of the banker-customer relationship changes over time.

The case of *Ahmed –v- Clydesdale Bank plc*[77] serves as an example. That was a case in which a wife sought reduction of a standard security which she had granted in 1991 insofar as affecting her interest in a flat owned by the pursuer and her husband. That security was entered into as a mortgage transaction to fund the purchase of the flat, but it was an "all sums" security and therefore apt to cover any other borrowing owed by either of the debtors to the bank.

In 1992 the pursuer's husband had purchased a shop premises using a loan from the bank. In 1995 he entered into a further term loan agreement in order to restructure his business debts. The pursuer was apparently entirely unaware of this activity. She was also unaware that

[77] 2001 SLT 423

the bank deemed the security over the flat to be security for this additional business lending.

At around this time – 1995 – the Bank had written to the pursuer stating that they understood she was willing to grant a guarantee on account of her husband's business debts. She was not so willing and she specifically advised the Bank as such. No formal personal guarantee was ever entered into.

The term loan was nonetheless advanced to the husband by the bank. This was a fact of which the pursuer was again unaware. In terms of the "all sums" provisions of the prior standard security, the term loan became secured and was looked to by the lender for the business loan. In effect, therefore, Mrs Ahmed was a cautioner for her husband's business notwithstanding she had refused to sign a formal guarantee.

It was argued for the pursuer that the lender was not in good faith as a result of:-

(a) Entering the term loan with her husband in the knowledge that it was effectively guaranteed by the security, and further in the knowledge that the pursuer had no desire to be a guarantor; and

(b) Failing to advise the pursuer that they had taken those steps, the effect of the security or that she should take independent legal advice.

Smith was relied upon by Mrs Ahmed in relation to the obligation of good faith. It was argued that the impression given to the pursuer by the letter inviting her to grant a guarantee was that if she did not so sign, she would not be liable as a guarantor. In fact, the advance of the loan would be secured by the pre-existing security and it was argued that the lender was under a duty to disclose that to her.

In his discussion, the Lord Ordinary stated that the starting point for consideration must be the deed which was being sought to reduce – the 1991 Security. The Lord Ordinary set out the issue as follows:-

"The context in which it was granted was the making of a loan by the defenders to the pursuer and her husband to finance the purchase by them of a house. They were to be joint owners of the house, and they were joint borrowers of the loan. It is therefore not surprising to find that they incurred a joint and several personal obligation, as well as burdening the subjects which they were jointly acquiring as security for the loan. This was therefore not the sort of situation dealt with in *Smith* and the cases which have followed it, where one spouse grants a standard security over her share in the matrimonial home in security of a debt owed to the lender by the other spouse alone. The form of the standard security, however, was not such as to confine the personal obligation undertaken to the repayment of the house purchase loan, or to provide heritable security only for that loan. Instead, the personal obligation was: "to pay ... all sums which are now and which may at any time hereafter become due to the Bank in any manner of way by ... us, either solely or jointly with any person or persons or corporation, company, firm or other body, and whether as principal or surety", and declaration (Ninth) added: "in the event of the personal obligation contained in this Standard Security being granted by more than one person, the said sums shall include all sums for which any one or more of the granters may now be or become liable to the Bank".

The security granted was of corresponding scope. The effect was that the pursuer there and then undertook a personal obligation in respect of all sums that her husband might at any time become liable to pay to the defenders, as well as granting a heritable security for all such liabilities over her interest in the security subjects. The pursuer thus committed herself in advance to being cautioner for her husband's future debts to the defenders, and extended the heritable security that she granted to cover all such debts. Counsel for the defenders was in my view correct in submitting that, since it was conceded that there were solicitors acting for the pursuer and her husband at the time when the standard security was granted, the defenders were entitled to

> suppose that the pursuer was advised as to those aspects of the effect of the standard security expressed as it was. It was not argued on the pursuer's behalf that there were any circumstances adversely affecting the validity of the standard security when it was granted."[78]

As a result, it was held that the point at which the bank must be in good faith is the time that the security is put in place. There was no additional duty incumbent upon the lender to advise the cautioner for every subsequent advance which is made.

This is a matter also considered by the Inner House *in Royal Bank of Scotland plc –v- Wilson.*[79] The view of Lord Osborne is worth setting out in full:

> "Looking at these statements of the circumstances in which a duty could arise upon the creditor, in my opinion, it is very hard to see how any such duty would arise in the context of the present cases. In each case, a personal obligation and standard security was executed jointly by a husband and wife for the purpose of the obtaining of finance from the pursuers for their own domestic purposes. There was no question of the husbands alone obtaining loans for their own purposes, with their liabilities being gratuitously guaranteed by their wives. No doubt, in these cases, the pursuers were well aware that the first and second defenders, in each case, were married and therefore enjoyed a close personal relationship. However, I can discern here no circumstances which would lead a reasonable man to believe that the consent of the wives to the transactions might not be fully informed or freely given. Indeed, having regard to the nature of the present transactions, it is difficult to regard the husbands as the principal debtors and the wives as the proposed cautioners. The fact of the matter is that each husband and wife were borrowing money

[78] *Ibid.,* at p.426

[79] 2004 SC 153

> jointly for their own domestic purposes. Accordingly, at the time of the transactions themselves, each husband and wife were simply joint debtors. In that context, it appears to me that the principles set forth by Lord Clyde [in Smith], taken their own terms, would not apply to the circumstances of these cases."[80]

It seems settled, therefore, that the Smith principle is only engaged at the time that the security is taken, and no additional duty arises upon further lending being advanced.

Special knowledge on the part of the lender

Whilst not strictly a "Smith type" case in the true sense, the concept of good faith was examined in the case of *Gibson -v- Royal Bank of Scotland plc,*[81] which had an unusual set of facts.

Mr & Mrs Gibson raised proceedings against the bank seeking reduction of a standard security in favour of the bank which had been granted by Mrs Gibson's ex-husband. The ex-husband had originally owned the property. In terms of a minute of agreement between he and the Gibsons he had agreed to grant an option to Mr and Mrs Gibson to purchase the property and had given them a lease meantime. The pursuers sought to exercise their option by notice in 2005. Before that transaction had been completed (and at a point when none of the foregoing was reflected in the public registers) the bank had been granted their security.

The Gibsons argued that the bank were not in good faith and that the security fell to be reduced as a consequence. It was averred that the bank were aware of the option agreement (although they were not aware of it having been exercised), and that this knowledge ought to have placed them on inquiry.

---

80 *Ibid.,* at p.170

81 [2009] CSOH 14

The bank went to debate on the question of reduction of the security. The court declined to omit the pursuers' averments on reduction of the security from probation. Whilst much of the judgment centres on property law and the so-called "offside goals rule",[82] it was held that the bank's knowledge of the option agreement might give them "constructive knowledge" of the fact that it had been exercised and that a completion date had been fixed. As such, the court allowed the latter to proceed to proof:

> "In their pleadings the.[pursuers] offer to prove that from an early date the Bank were aware of the existence of the option agreement, and that as a matter of good faith and fair dealing this gave rise to an obligation to inquire into its nature and result. In my opinion it cannot be said that these averments reflect an approach which is necessarily wrong in law, nor one which would not be capable, after proof, of fixing the Bank with constructive knowledge..."[83]

It appears that care must therefore be taken by a lender. They must examine the whole of their knowledge about a transaction and weigh up the facts which are within their knowledge which might put them on inquiry. If inquiry is warranted, those inquiries must be made in order to maintain good faith.

Must the guarantee be gratuitous?

Thus far we have examined cases where the wife is taken to have little or no interest in the business, and therefore has (or has been assumed to have) had no benefit from the transaction. It may therefore be questioned whether the situation is different where the guarantor has a financial interest, even if tangential, in the business in question.

---

[82] See *Rodger (Builders) Ltd -v- Fawdry* 1950 SC 483

[83] *Ibid* at para [35]

In *Wright –v- Cotias Investments*[84] the facts were slightly different from the typical "Smith-type" case in that the pursuer was a mother who entered into a business arrangement with a third party, seemingly in an effort to save her son's business following his bankruptcy. The business arrangement was in the manner of a partnership, whereby the mother and third party would be equal shareholders, but the pursuer's son would run the business. The third party took the lead in making arrangements for the setting up of the business. It was he who arranged finance for the business, apparently through an associate of his, and took the leading role in the running of the business.

The pursuer had been a silent partner in the son's business previously and had significant liabilities as a result of that arrangement. The finance obtained by the third party amounted to £200,000, of which £155,000 went towards secured debts for which the pursuer was liable under her previous association with her son. The remainder went to the new business, of which the pursuer was a 50% shareholder.

The pursuer granted a guarantee in favour of the defender, an investment company, and a standard security over premises owned by her from which the business traded. This was to secure finance from the defender which had been arranged by the third party.

Perhaps inevitably, the business failed and the pursuer was threatened with being pursued by the defender. She sought reduction of the Guarantee and security on grounds that she was not given the requisite advice by the lender prior to granting them, thus rendering them in bad faith, and that she had entered into the transaction as a result of undue influence and a misrepresentation on the part of her son and the third party.

Having identified that this was an attempt to bring the case within the *Smith* principle, and examining that principle in some detail, the Lord Ordinary considered the question of whether bad faith alone was

---

84 2001 SLT 353

sufficient to found reduction. His conclusion was the same as Lord Hamilton's in *Braithwaite* – without an actionable wrong, there could be no reduction.

Having established that principle, the Lord Ordinary then went on to look at the nature of the transaction itself. He observes:

> "Although the pursuer avers that the loan transaction and the undertaking of the related cautionary obligations offered her no personal advantage on an objective view… she admits that of the £200,000 advanced, £155,000 was used to repay her secured creditors. Whatever may have happened thereafter, the loan was made to a company of which she was a director and in which she held 50% of the issued share capital"[85]

The personal interest which the pursuer held in the business and her financial interest in the transaction were matters of importance to the result. The Lord Ordinary concludes by saying:

> "In my view, however, the circumstances of the present case are not such as to entitle the pursuer to invoke the rule in *Smith v Bank of Scotland*. The circumstances which, in my view, combine to yield that result are (1) that the loan was necessary to refinance an existing business, (2) that, albeit the pursuer avers that she was not actively involved in the business, the debts of that business were debts for which she was personally liable, (3) that the premises which belonged to the pursuer were the subject of heritable securities in respect of the debts of the business, (4) that the interest of the pursuer's son in the business was only that of an employee and was thus much less direct than her own, (5) that the refinancing package was designed to enable the pursuer's existing borrowing to be repaid and the existing heritable securities over her property to be discharged, (6) that as part of that package Bond was set up and the pursuer became the holder

[85] *Ibid.*, at p.359

> of 50 per cent of the issued share capital, as well as a director of the company, (7) that the guarantee which the pursuer granted was thus a guarantee of the indebtedness of a company of which she was to the extent of 50 per cent the beneficial owner, and (8) the standard security which she granted was in security of the loan made to that company. Assuming that, as the pursuer avers, the proposed arrangement had been explained in detail to the defenders, I am of opinion that the circumstances are not such as to be capable of leading them, as reasonable men, to believe that owing to the personal relationship between the pursuer and her son her consent to the granting of the guarantee and the standard security might not be fully informed or freely given."[86]

Whilst the Lord Ordinary does venture that this is not a straightforward mother/son nor indeed director/shareholder case, he nevertheless concludes that the case does not fall within *Smith*.

A similar approach was taken by the temporary judge in the unreported case of *Christie –v- Bank of Scotland*.[87]

In that case a wife sought reduction of a personal guarantee and a standard security granted by she and her husband over the family home in relation to debts of a business run primarily by her husband, but in which she was a director and shareholder. It was averred that the deeds were granted gratuitously and that her consent was given under concealment of the nature and consequences of the documents and in circumstances where the lender ought reasonably to have suspected that her consent was so obtained.

It was averred that she had no recollection of signing the guarantee documentation, but admitted that her signature appeared on it. In

---

[86] *Ibid.*, at p.361

[87] Unreported, Opinion of Temp Judge TG Coutts QC, 29 August 2003

relation to the security she averred that this was signed under psychological pressure from her husband.

In considering the question before him, the temporary judge adopted the line of reasoning set out in *Wilson* – a case we shall examine in more detail below – looking firstly at whether there was a cautionary obligation, secondly whether it was gratuitous and finally at whether there is relevantly averred any misrepresentation and any breach of the duty of good faith.

At paragraph [23] of the judgment he concludes as follows:-

> "In relation to the Personal Guarantee it is difficult to view that as gratuitous since it was a guarantee given by the directors and secretary of the company in relation to the company debts. Both husband and wife had a clear interest in the maintenance of the company and in any event the Personal Guarantee was not in order to relieve the husband of obligations but to share the consequences of obligations incurred or to be incurred by the company."

At Paragraph [28] the temporary judge goes on to say:-

> "The defenders were in a position where the directors and secretary of the limited liability company gave a personal guarantee for the debts of that company. There is nothing unusual in that. The bank knew that they were both participants in the company and that this was not simply a case of a wife giving a guarantee for her husband's debts. No further inquiry was, in my view, required in relation to the personal guarantee".

The question of whether a transaction is gratuitous was also raised in *Royal Bank of Scotland –v- Wilson.*[88] *Wilson* was in fact two cases involving two brothers and their respective spouses. The brothers and

[88] 2004 SC 153

spouses each entered into a loan agreement with the Bank – one for the purposes of purchasing their property, and the other for the purposes of building a conservatory. In both cases those loans were secured by a standard security over their respective properties.

Some time later, the brothers – who were in partnership in a business – obtained borrowings from the Bank in relation to that business. Those facilities went into default and the bank sought to enforce their security. In this respect the situation was similar to that of Mrs Ahmed.

The wives claimed that they had been misled into believing that the standard securities secured only the loans which they had taken out, and they were unaware that they could be liable for subsequent borrowings. It was argued that in making them cautioners for their respective husbands, the security went far beyond the immediate purpose of each transaction and the duty of good faith was accordingly breached from the outset on the basis that no solicitor would reasonably advise their client to grant such a security.

Following procedure and appeals in the courts below, the matter was heard before the Second Division of the Inner House. It was held that the obligations which the wives had entered into had not been entered gratuitously and that there was no relevant case of bad faith.

In relation to that first finding, the Lord Justice Clerk (as he then was) puts the matter succinctly in his opinion:

> "Counsel for the second defenders presented these as cases about the duty of good faith owed by the pursuer in circumstances where by granting the security the wife became liable for any subsequent borrowings from the pursuer by her husband and got nothing in return; but that is an incomplete view. Under these securities, the husband incurred an equally onerous potential liability in respect of any borrowings from the pursuer by the wife. Each spouse secured the debts of the other.

> [24] In my opinion, these appeals fail on the ground that the second defenders did not incur the cautionary obligation gratuitously. In incurring a cautionary obligation in respect of her husband's future debts, each received the benefit of a co-extensive obligation on his part in respect of her own. In *Smith v Bank of Scotland* the discussion seems to have proceeded on the assumption that the wife incurred a cautionary obligation in respect of her husband's debts and got nothing in return. The Session papers in *Smith v Bank of Scotland* show that the standard security was an all-sums security in similar terms to these, but this point was not taken in that case. In my view, it is a decisive point in the present cases. "[89]

It accordingly appears settled that where a guarantee is not given gratuitously, the protection afforded to the spouse in *Smith* will not be available.

Before moving on, it is worth taking notice of the case of *Cooper -v- Bank of Scotland plc*[90] That was a case where it was proved that the pursuer's husband had misrepresented the position to the pursuer, and that the pursuer had been unaware that she had been appointed as company secretary. The court held that the evidence showed that the pursuer disapproved of her husband's business venture and would not have signed a security had she understood the import of the document. The court held that the pursuer was entitled to reduction. To the writer's knowledge it is the only successful action of this type since *Smith.*

There are a couple of oddities about the case. It appears to have been accepted that the Bank had not given the warning and enjoined the pursuer to seek legal advice, but it is likely given the date of the security in this question that such a warning would have been clear from the deed itself.[91] Moreover the court placed some weight on the fact that the

---

[89] *Ibid.,* at p.159

[90] [2014] CSOH 16

[91] cf. *Clydesdale Bank plc -v-Black*, 2002 SC 555

pursuer was unaware of her appointment as Company Secretary, however it is difficult to square this with the fact that the Inner House has held a Bank has no duty to carry out its own investigations into the background.[92]

Cooper has been criticised,[93] and might be readily distinguishable. However, it does suggest that it is not sufficient for a lender to take the cautioner's apparent position within a business at face value.

What constitutes "undue influence"?

We have seen in previous cases that the concept of what constitutes undue influence can be hard to pin down in Scots law. *Broadway –v- Clydesdale Bank plc (No.2)*[94] was a case which considered the question of what constitutes undue influence. The evidence bore to show that the pursuer's husband had placed a document before her saying that she should sign it and that it was all right to do so as her personal assets would not be at risk. In fact the document was a standard security which burdened her share of her home.

The case turns to a large degree on its facts, but that is really the point. Under Scots law there is no presumption of undue influence and it will therefore require to be proved. That may set a higher bar than a spouse might need to meet south of the border. The Lord Ordinary's summation of the position within the family is worth setting out in full:

> "[in matters of business] it was the pursuer who reposed trust and confidence in Leslie [the husband] to such an extent that he was in a position to exercise influence over her. The question therefore comes to be whether he did so in relation to her granting the standard security. The contention for the pursuer is

[92] *Ibid.*, as discussed below. 2014 SLT 185

[93] See C. Anderson, "Cautionary wives again: Cooper v Bank of Scotland",

[94] 2003 SLT 707

that he did so by asking her to sign it, and telling her that it was all right to do so, when in fact it put her interest in Westquarter at risk. I have accepted the pursuer's evidence that Leslie did tell her that it was all right to sign the standard security (see para 13 above). I do not consider that, apart from the question of whether it was "all right" for her to sign it, Leslie has been proved to have misled the pursuer or otherwise abused his influence over her. I accept that he explained to her that the loan was the responsibility of Anthony and Sandra, but in terms of the personal obligation that was correct. The pursuer knew that security would be required, and although her understanding was that it would affect only [her son]'s share of Westquarter, it was not alleged that Leslie said that that would be so. I do not consider that his statement that it would be "all right" to sign the security can be taken as a false indication that it would not affect the whole of Westquarter. It is clear that Leslie understood that the security was over the whole of Westquarter. It seems to me, however, that the evidence does not exclude the possibility that in saying to the pursuer that it was "all right" to sign the security, what he was intending to convey was that on balance there was no unacceptable risk. While on a strict analysis, the granting of the security was to the pursuer's disadvantage in that she put her share of Westquarter at risk with no corresponding benefit to herself, I do not consider that it is likely that it occurred to Leslie to view the matter in that formal way. In the first place, Westquarter was the family home, both for him and the pursuer and for Anthony and Sandra. Title had originally stood in his name. The various dispositions which yielded the result that one half share belonged to Anthony and one quarter share belonged to the pursuer were, on the evidence, undertaken for inheritance tax planning reasons. In the second place, the company was a family asset. It had been built up by Leslie and the pursuer and had provided for them and their family over the years, and had latterly been passed over into the management of the younger generation of the family, to provide their living in turn. The

> purpose of the borrowing from the defenders was to enable that family business to continue and expand. It seems to me that it is likely that Leslie regarded that as a desirable family objective which justified the provision of support in the form of allowing the family home to be burdened in security. The evidence before me does not enable me to form any opinion as to the magnitude of the risk, as perceived in October 1992, that the defenders would have occasion to enforce the standard security by selling Westquarter. It therefore seems to me that, while there was undoubtedly a risk for the pursuer individually which was not balanced by any personal benefit, it cannot be said to have been proved that, when the transaction was viewed from the perspective of the family as a whole, it was untenable to regard it as the right and appropriate thing to do. Leslie evidently thought it was the right thing to do, since he burdened his own remaining quarter share of Westquarter in exactly the same way as the pursuer did hers. I do not consider that the difference in shareholding between the pursuer and Leslie is in the context a factor that materially distinguishes the risks which they respectively took"[95]

Thus one needs more than a whiff of wrongdoing. If the alleged misrepresentation by the husband might in fact be considered true (or at least not entirely untruthful) it may not avail the cautioner of a remedy.

Thomson -v- Royal Bank of Scotland plc[96] is another case in which the behaviour of the husband was examined in order to determine whether it amounted to an actionable wrong. In that case there was no suggestion of the husband exercising a domineering or dominant influence over the wife. He was, however, the sole breadwinner in the household and had concealed from her the extent of his financial difficulties. Certainly the

---

[95] *Ibid.,* at p.720

[96] 2003 SC 964

wife trusted the husband in financial matters and, when presented with the security for signature, she signed without question.

It appears that the pursuer had not been legally represented and had not been given the requisite "Smith" advice by the Bank. The husband had failed to fully inform his wife as to what she was signing and of the extent of his financial difficulties. The question was whether the concealment on the part of the husband amounted to an actionable wrong which would render the bank's security vulnerable to reduction.

It was held that there was no authority for the proposition that undue influence could arise simply from a failure by the husband to voluntarily disclose information to his wife which had not been asked for:

> "… senior counsel for the pursuer ultimately sought to persuade me that undue influence could arise simply from a failure by the husband to volunteer information about the transaction, which had not been asked for and/or to direct the wife that she should obtain independent legal advice in relation to the transaction. While such an approach, if adopted, would be good news to lawyers, and while it was advanced forcefully in the present case, there is simply no warrant in either principle or authority for it in the law of Scotland."[97]

It can accordingly be seen that a careful analysis is required as to what the misrepresentation by the debtor to his or her spouse is said to be. The factual matrix will be important in determining that question, and establishing undue influence will depend on the facts and circumstances of each case viewed in its context. Cases will turn on their own facts.

---

[97] *Ibid.*, at p.994

Does the "Etridge" Principle apply in Scotland?

We have seen that the House of Lords in the English case of *Etridge (No.2)* imposed a prescriptive regime which both lenders and solicitors were to follow in order to ensure that the lender did not have constructive notice of undue influence. This involved specification of the advice which must be given and the information to be exchanged between lender and solicitor. To date, attempts to import this prescriptive approach into Scots law have failed.

Clydesdale Bank plc -v- Black[98] is one example. We have considered the facts above. In the result, the court rejected the *Etridge* approach, and determined that all a lender required to follow were the steps set out by Lord Clyde in *Smith* – to warn of the consequences and to advise the cautioner to take legal advice. In the words of Lord Marnoch:

> "... there is, in my opinion, no place for the sort of investigation envisaged by their Lordships' House in *Royal Bank of Scotland plc v Etridge (No 2)*. Nor, indeed, is the emphasis necessarily on 'bringing home' to the wife the risks she was running by standing as surety. Unlike England, there is no requirement for the creditor to 'shed' the constructive notice which might otherwise be imputed to him. On the contrary, as Lord Clyde puts the matter in *Smith* (at p 122): 'Whether there has in fact been or may yet be any conduct by the debtor directed at the cautioner which might vitiate the contract is not a matter necessarily to be explored by the creditor. All that is required of him is that *he* should take reasonable steps to secure that in relation to the proposed contract *he* acts throughout in good faith' (my italics). In short, as I see it, all that is requisite in Scotland is that, in the course of his communings with the cautioner, in addition to compliance with the duties already incumbent upon him under the earlier law, the creditor should now 'warn the potential cautioner of the consequences of entering into the proposed

[98] 2002 SC 555

> cautionary obligation and… advise him or her to take independent advice'—*Smith* at p 122. As it happens, these same steps are again referred to by Lord Clyde in *Royal Bank of Scotland plc v Etridge (No 2)* at p. 1051, and I see no suggestion there that, for Scotland, the position should be regarded as having in any way altered. In particular, there is no suggestion that the duty which Lord Clyde identified in *Smith* should now be seen, contrary to what was said in *Smith*, 'to carry with it a duty of investigation'."[99]

Lord Sutherland, having examined in full the passage from Lord Clyde's speech in the *Etridge* case similarly concludes:

> "Obviously it has to be borne in mind that Lord Clyde's decision to agree in the result [in *Etridge*] was taken in the context of English law. Furthermore, the comments which he makes as to the steps which have to be taken by a lender are also to be seen in the context of English law. I have quoted this passage in full to ascertain if there can be discerned any departure referable to Scots law from what he said in *Smith*. Having considered the matter carefully I am satisfied not only that he did not seek to extend (or further 'develop') the law of Scotland but that he confirms what he said in *Smith*. I am therefore satisfied that *Etridge* makes no practical difference to the law of Scotland. In any event, again, it is difficult to see how it could have any bearing on whether or not the respondents acted in good faith in 1996. I do not consider that any inference can be drawn from what Lord Clyde said either in *Smith* or in *Etridge* that he was of opinion that in Scotland there was or should be a duty to investigate how far the written warnings and advice had been seen, understood and followed up by a guarantor and thereby 'satisfy' themselves that all was well. To achieve such satisfaction would in my view require a lender to indulge in investigation of the type which it is agreed he has no duty to carry out. It follows that I am of opinion that the defender

---

[99] *Ibid.*, at p.570

> and appellant has failed to aver any relevant basis for saying that the pursuers and respondents failed in any duty owed by them to her, and that accordingly this appeal should be refused."[100]

It appears tolerably clear, therefore, that the prescriptive requirements of *Etridge* do not apply in the law of Scotland.

100 *Ibid.,* at p.573

CHAPTER SIX

THE CURRENT STATE OF THE LAW

In the previous chapter we examined the development of the law following the decision in *Smith*. In this chapter the intention is to pull this together into a coherent statement of the law as it currently stands.

We have seen that following *Smith* there was a lengthy period of retrenchment within the law. Fences were erected around the *Smith* principle, penning it in and distinguishing it from the developments south of the border to ensure that the core of Scots law was unaffected by the potential contagion.

Two things are notable. First, it took almost two decades following *Smith* for a court in Scotland to uphold a challenge to Bank documentation based on *Smith* principles.[101] Second, it can be seen that the more eye-catching developments of the principle south of the border – the extension to employer/employee relationships, for example[102] – have largely been either untested or resisted in Scotland.

We will look in more detail at the *Cooper* case in the next Chapter where consideration will be given to potential future developments. In this Chapter we will look to set out in reasonably brief terms the scope of the Smith principle as it currently stands.

Good faith

We have seen that the concept of good faith is central to the line of cases. What emerges is that the bar in Scotland is relatively low as regards how

101 *Cooper -v- Bank of Scotland plc* [2014] CSOH 16

102 *Credit Lyonnais Bank Nederland NV -v- Burch* [1997] 1 All ER 144

a lender can engage in a transaction and remain in good faith. What a bank requires to do is:

- Explain the consequences of the transaction in question; and
- Advise the cautioner to obtain independent legal advice.

In modern banking documentation, both of those elements are generally printed onto the front of the deed itself making it very difficult for a bank to act in bad faith. That said, there may be cases in which these warnings are not given. What then is the bank's position?

First, it must be noted that the bank's good faith is measured at the time that the obligation is entered into. A domestic mortgage transaction based on an "all sums security" may not engage the *Smith* principle. However nor does the principle become engaged in relation to that security at a later date if business borrowing is advanced which was not envisaged at the time of the mortgage lending. If the bank was in good faith at the time of the transaction they remain in good faith for most purposes thereafter.

The authorities show that in a number of cases a bank might still argue that the transaction is valid where the advice is not given. Hence:

- The lender will remain in good faith if the cautioner is represented by a solicitor in the transaction, even if that solicitor is acting for more than one party;
- A breach of the requirement of good faith will in any event not invalidate the transaction unless there is an actionable wrong on the part of the principal debtor. That wrong must be proven, and each case will turn upon its own facts in that regard.
- Likewise, where the transaction is not entered gratuitously by the guarantor a breach of the requirement of good faith will not necessarily invalidate the transaction. The bar is set quite high

here, and the Inner House have held that entering into an "all sums" Standard Security will produce a co-extensive cautionary obligation each spouse to the other. Such a transaction may not therefore be gratuitous even if that co-extensive obligation is more theoretical than real.

Investigations and Constructive Notice

The law of England in this area is based largely on the concept of "constructive notice". The steps which a lender requires to take are therefore in place to prevent them from being "fixed" with knowledge of a spouse's wrongdoing.

The House in *Smith* considered whether the same principle of constructive notice could be imported into Scotland to extend the law. Lord Clyde appeared to consider it a possibility, but preferred the solution of extending "good faith". That is a major conceptual difference borne of the difference in underlying legal concepts within each jurisdiction.[103] Ultimately this different basis has had a profound effect on the development of the law and has been a major factor in the divergence of Scots and English law.

One consequence of the use of good faith as a base has been that being in good faith will rarely, if ever, fix the lender with notice of actual wrongdoing on the part of their borrower. That means that the courts in Scotland have readily held that a lender has no duty to make their own investigations at the time that the transaction is completed. Two effects of that, which differ from English law, are:

1. The lender in Scotland has no interest in the actual advice which is given to the cautioner, and does not require the solicitor to confirm to them what that advice entails; and

[103] The concept of "good faith" in a contract under English law is considered in *Yam Seng Pte Ltd -v- International Trade Corp Limited* [2013] 1 All ER (Comm) 1321

2. The lender's duty to the cautioner is discharged by giving them a warning to take independent legal advice on the transaction. The lender in Scotland has no duty whatsoever to *ensure* that the cautioner obtains advice, and it is wholly a matter for the spouse if they do not wish to take such advice.

For these reasons, the more prescriptive requirements for solicitors and lenders set out in *Etridge (no.2)* have been rejected in Scotland.

Writing -v- Verbal warnings

We saw in *O'Brien* that the House of Lords considered it important that the advice set out in that case should be given by the lender to the surety in a face-to-face meeting. It was recognised in *Etridge (No.2)* that there was a reticence on the part of lenders to do so for two main reasons: first, the lender had no desire to take responsibility for the advice given and preferred to pass this responsibility to solicitors; and second, that the lender wished to avoid a situation where it is claimed that something was said in such a meeting, verbally, which was not recorded but which would (if proved) affect the lender's prospects of success. As a result, the lenders relied heavily upon legal advice given to sureties in these cases.

In Scotland, *Smith* did not specify that the advice required to be given in person. In fact Lord Clyde implicitly approved the code of practice of lenders at this time, which had such a warning in writing on the face of the deed. We have seen that subsequent cases have upheld that such written warnings will be held to be sufficient.

There is, of course, room for argument that the warnings were not read or were not understood.

In relation to a case based on lack of understanding of the printed warning, there is no real authority on this point. It is suggested that the test is an objective one – what would a person of reasonable mental acuity understand from the printed warnings. In the majority of cases the warnings are very clear and highlighted in bold type. It is suggested that a case based on lack of understanding, in the absence of special knowledge on the part of the bank, would be difficult to sustain.

But what if the warning is not read? In cases of this type, it is often said that information was hidden from the guarantor by their spouse. It is not beyond the realms of possibility that a rogue spouse might hide the relevant warning from his or her spouse as part of a scheme to induce their signature. If the guarantor is not represented, this might pose a difficulty for the lender – they cannot show that they gave the relevant advice to the guarantor as they cannot show that it was available for them to read. In those circumstances it is possible that a claim for reduction based on *Smith* might succeed. There has not, however, been a reported case where those facts have been in issue. We return to this theme in the next chapter.

There is also, of course, a major difference between the warning being concealed from the guarantor as set out above, and the guarantor making a choice not to read the deed which has been presented to them for signature. It is suggested that in the latter case, it would be very difficult for a cautioner to sustain a case against the lender.

The value of *Smith*

Given the apparent difficulties for a cautioner in sustaining a claim against a bank for reduction of a cautionary obligation, and the relatively low bar (compared to England & Wales) for a lender to meet their obligations, it might be questioned whether the *Smith* principle has any value in modern transactions.

That question is not straightforward to answer.

In the first place *Smith* remains an important additional protection for a spouse where either the lender or the borrower is a rogue. The *Smith* principle specifically does not give the lender a license to be wilfully blind. If there are facts or circumstances known to a lender which would give rise to further inquiry as to whether the spouse's consent is freely given, the lender cannot ignore those facts and must take steps to remain in good faith. In that sense, *Smith* still has value.

Moreover, there will remain cases in which the lender wholly fails to give the required advice. This is particularly so given the prevalence of new lenders into the market where documentation may be being drafted from scratch. In those circumstances the lender would have no protection where an actionable wrong on the part of the borrower is uncovered. That such cases will be few and far between does not dilute the power of the principle, and may equally be testament to improvements in banking practice over the past 25 years.

In fact, the success of the *O'Brien* and *Etridge (No.2)* principles in England, coupled with the rise of cross-border lenders, standardised banking practices and standard documentation is almost certainly the reason why so few cases have been successful. Most major lenders operate on both sides of the border. It therefore makes commercial sense to have a single process to follow where such lends are made. Most lenders opt to follow the most onerous process, being that in place south of the border. As a result, a large number of lends made in Scotland which might be affected by *Smith* are put in place with the *Etridge* principles in mind. As such, they go far beyond the requirements of Scots law and are rendered difficult to challenge unless there has been a significant breakdown of the process.

The danger for lenders with such an approach, however, is that in following *Etridge* principles in Scotland they take on more responsibility than they are required to. This may in turn lead to the lender uncovering facts which put them on inquiry when they might not otherwise be. That might result in unintended consequences in the right circumstances – the lender can't ignore special circumstances, and it is well established that a misrepresentation on the part of a lender can found an action for reduction, even where there was no general duty upon the lender to disclose the misrepresented facts.[104]

[104] *Royal Bank of Scotland -v- O'Donnell* 2015 SC 258

CHAPTER SEVEN

FUTURE BATTLEGROUNDS

Reference was made above to the case of *Cooper -v- Bank of Scotland plc.*[105] As mentioned, this case is the only major example of the *Smith* principle being applied in favour of the cautioner. It came almost two decades after *Smith* and a good 15 or more years after most of the issues we have discussed above had been settled. As such, it is an important reminder that *Smith* remains a live issue and is a useful starting point to consider what the future may hold for litigation in this area.

Cooper

The story of Mr and Mrs Cooper begins with the purchase of two adjacent plots of land by Mr and Mrs Cooper and their son respectively for the purpose of building their homes. Mr Cooper and his son later discovered an artesian well on the son's property and decided that this may become a lucrative enterprise. They formed a company of which each of Mr Cooper Senior and Junior held a 50% share. Their object was to bottle and distribute the water from their well. The judgment records that Mrs Cooper was not enthusiastic about the business venture.

In 2002 Mr and Mrs Cooper granted a standard security over their home as part of a remortgage transaction. The standard security was an "all sums" security covering all debts due and that might become due in the future from either party.

As the judgment of the Lord Ordinary records:

> "At about that time Mr Cooper and his son decided, despite the pursuer's resistance, to take their water bottling business plans forward. They obtained an overdraft for Burnswell [the business]

105 [2014] CSOH 16

> from the defenders (and a small start-up grant from the local authority) to fund the set-up costs of the company's business. They purchased equipment and began to pump and bottle water from the well. They took stalls at trade shows and attracted interest in their product. However, in order to progress the business they required an external investor. None was forthcoming and, as time went on, the amount of Burnswell's overdraft steadily increased."[106]

In due course the bank required that Mr Cooper and his son grant personal guarantees, which they duly did. Later, Mr Cooper's son left the business and Mr Cooper signed a further personal guarantee taking on all of the debts of the business up to £75,000, and then later still a further guarantee for £80,000.

So far the case is virtually indistinguishable from cases such as *Wilson* and *Ahmed.* A standard security undertaken for mortgage purposes which is later held for subsequent business borrowing. For aught yet seen, there was no case for the bank to answer. However the case was about to take a twist.

In about 2006 the Coopers sought to remortgage their home to Halifax plc, and the bank instructed a firm of solicitors to act on their behalf in that remortgage transaction. The firm of solicitors had been told that the security over the property was being held for business purposes in addition to the domestic mortgage, but appear to have overlooked that direction. They signed (under power of attorney) a discharge of that security in return for payment of the mortgage loan only. A first-ranked security was then put in place in favour of Halifax plc.

There appeared to be some discussion around Mrs Cooper becoming guarantor, which did not progress. At some point Mrs Cooper was appointed as Company Secretary, albeit she claimed in evidence to have had no knowledge of that appointment. In 2007 the bank's solicitor

[106] *Ibid.*, at para [4]

wrote to the Coopers explaining that "[t]he Bank of Scotland confirm that although your residential mortgage account has been transferred to Halifax plc, the Bank have a continuing requirement to hold a security over your property for business borrowings". A fresh security was sent to the Coopers for signature to "replace[…] the similar document signed by you in 2002". This bears to have been signed and returned, as it was recorded in the register in 2007.

It does not appear that Mrs Cooper was given information on the import of the security and nor was she encouraged to obtain independent legal advice.[107] In 2011 Mr Cooper appears to have admitted to his solicitor that Mrs Cooper knew nothing of the business debts, nor of his personal guarantee. It is not clear from the judgment how much was known of the granting of the fresh standard security in 2007.

In 2012 the bank called up the security and Mrs Cooper raised her action seeking reduction of the security.

According to Mrs Cooper's evidence:

> "Mr Cooper presented her with a document in early 2007 and asked her to sign it. He told her that the document related to 'the mortgage' and that the payments would increase. According to the pursuer's understanding, Mr Cooper's reference to "the mortgage" was to their home loan, and the reason for the increase in the monthly payments was to pay off this loan more quickly, which she regarded as a good idea. Mr Cooper showed her only the page that she had to sign. She did not read the document before signing it."[108]

[107] As noted above, most standard security documentation now contains this wording in bold type and/or capital letters as standard at the head or foot of the security. This has been held sufficient in other cases to satisfy the requirement, but if that wording was present on this security the point does not appear to have been taken.

[108] *Ibid.,* at para [18]

Mrs Cooper trusted her husband in financial matters and had no reason to disbelieve him. Unusually in this type of case, Mr Cooper also gave evidence and admitted to having concealed the true situation from his wife. He had concealed correspondence and had not told her about the business debt nor the personal guarantee. When his son resigned from the business he appointed his wife company secretary without telling her. The court accepted this evidence.

Turning to the test in *Smith* the Lord Ordinary held that this was a three-part test: first, was the obligation gratuitous; second, has an actionable wrong been committed; and third, were the lenders in good faith?

Whilst the 2002 security was clearly not granted gratuitously, it was conceded by the bank that the 2007 security was gratuitous on the part of Mrs Cooper. The Court having accepted Mr and Mrs Cooper's evidence as to his wrongdoing, the second part of the test was also satisfied. That left the question of good faith.

The court held that the bank were not in good faith. It was said that they had not taken any steps either themselves or through their agents to bring home to Mrs Cooper the consequences of the transaction. Nor was she cautioned to take independent legal advice. The letter from the bank's solicitors was "in bland terms" and gave the impression that the security was a formality. The court had little doubt that if Mrs Cooper knew the true position she would not have signed.

As a consequence, Mrs Cooper was successful, and the security was reduced. It does not appear that the result was appealed by the bank.

Lessons from Cooper

At first glance *Cooper* may appear to turn on its facts. Certainly, it is highly unusual for a husband to testify against his own interests, but there are a number of factors which might lead one to re-evaluate some of the post-Smith case law. It is possible that these areas may form future battlegrounds for Smith-type litigation.

The Bank's duty of investigation

As has been established, the bank's duty to maintain good faith does not encompass a duty to undertake their own investigations. That has been identified as being a side-effect of the Scottish principle being based on good faith whilst the English principle is based on "constructive notice" which a lender requires to "shed".[109] There may be an exception to that rule where the lender has knowledge which puts them on inquiry, but otherwise the rule is relatively hard and fast.

In *Cooper* however, there did not appear to be any suggestion that the bank had particular knowledge as to Mrs Cooper's attitude to the business nor her lack of knowledge of the extent of the business debts. Moreover there appears to have been no suggestion that the bank knew or ought to have known of the extent of Mr Cooper's deception, or that she had been appointed as company secretary without her knowledge. There was nothing in the established facts which might be thought to have put the bank on inquiry so that they ought to undertake investigations.

On the other hand, it clearly was known to the bank that Mrs Cooper was the company secretary in a trading business. Moreover, whilst the letter from the bank's solicitors was perhaps sub-optimal, it did refer clearly to business debts. In those circumstances it is unclear how the bank could have been alerted to the husband's wrongdoing in the absence of further investigation. In addition, it is unclear how the bank could have been aware that the wife did not have a financial interest in the business (notwithstanding that she held the position of company secretary) without further investigation.

If *Cooper* was correctly decided[110] therefore it may be seen as tentative authority for the proposition that a lender might have to make further

[109] See Chapter 4, above.

[110] It should be borne in mind that *Cooper* is a judgment of the Lord Ordinary at first instance, and is not binding.

investigations to establish good faith, even though they have no positive duty to do so and may have no special knowledge to prompt them to do so. The trigger for those investigations is uncertain, and so it is possible that future case law may be required to clarify this issue.

The effect of written warnings and advice

We have seen above that the use of written warnings and advice to the cautioner has been held as sufficient to meet the *Smith* test.

In this case there is no reference in the judgment of any warning having been present on the security documentation signed by Mrs Cooper. The letter from the bank's solicitor did not contain advice on the nature of the transaction and did not recommend that she seek legal advice. As mentioned above, it would have been unusual at this point in time for a standard security not to have made reference to the nature of the obligation it represented and for it to contain a recommendation to seek independent advice.

In practical terms, written warnings would have availed Mrs Cooper very little, as it was found in fact that she had not read the letter nor the terms of the security. It was found that the signing page of the security had been "presented" to her and the letter had been concealed from her entirely by her husband.

The question is whether the lender requires to be satisfied that the cautioner has in fact read the warnings in question when they are given in writing, or whether it is sufficient to assume that correspondence addressed to a party will be given to that party. *Cooper* does not assist with that question, and the cases in which the warnings were given in writing do not specifically deal with the issue of what might happen if those warnings were actively concealed from the cautioner by a rogue spouse. Technically if the warnings are concealed then it is arguable that no warning or advice has been given. However, this must be balanced against the fact that the bank might not have any reason to doubt that the warnings have been read and has no additional duty of investigation.

If a lender requires to check that a warning has been read, that comes dangerously close to an *Etridge* style duty upon the bank.

Again, this area might prove to be a battleground of the future for spouses seeking a remedy.

The effect of an error on the part of the bank

A feature of *Cooper* was that it was the bank's (or at least their agent's) error in discharging the 2002 security which led to the issue.

There seems little room for doubt that if the 2002 security had not been discharged then the principle in *Ahmed* as affirmed by the Inner House in *Wilson* would have rendered that security enforceable in relation to the business debt. The 2007 security was specifically referred to in the solicitors' letter as being to "replace" the 2002 security.

It was conceded by the bank that the 2007 security was gratuitous. Presumably the 2002 security was not. The difference between the two is likely to have been that the 2002 security secured a mortgage loan of which Mrs Cooper was a co-recipient. It is that joint borrowing which is presumed to have prevented the security being gratuitous.

Two points arise:

1. Should a cautioner be entitled to take advantage of the bank's error in this way and improve her position accordingly?; and
2. Was the 2007 security truly gratuitous?

In relation to the first point, the starting point is that the security from 2002 was apt to cover the business lending. In that sense the discharge should never have been granted. In those circumstances, does the lender who had a valid security for their business debt require to comply with *Smith* where that security has been discharged in error and a replacement security is signed?

It would be arguable that the lender should be held in good faith on the basis that the cautioner's position on signing the new security in 2007 would have been precisely the same as her position up to the moment the discharge of the 2002 security was registered earlier that year. If the bank were in good faith and had the ability to recover under the security up to 16th January 2007 (when the discharge was registered) what logical reason is there to hold them not to be in good faith on 26th April 2007 when the new security was recorded. All that had happened was that they were rectifying their error. In those circumstances it might be argued that *Smith* should not apply at all. The cautioner had received a windfall, and should not be entitled to take advantage of that.

On the other hand it is equally arguable that *Smith* should apply. The fact that a domestic mortgage had been the main object of the original 2002 security was the reason why the bank had protection in the first place. If they no longer held obligations payable by both parties to the security, it would make some sense for the bank to have a duty to advise the spouse as to the nature of the obligation as it now stands. As examined above, good faith must be measured at the time of the transaction in question, and the bank's error is not necessarily relevant where a new security is being entered into.

That leads to the second point – whether the security was truly gratuitous. We have seen that *Smith* only applies where the cautioner has no financial interest in the transaction whatsoever. A security which covers a domestic mortgage payable by both spouses is one example of a transaction which would not be gratuitous, because the security would be in relation to a debt owed by both parties, even if one has additional borrowing on top.

However in *Wilson* the Inner House concluded that the security in that case was not gratuitously given. The Lord Justice Clerk, it will be recalled, opined that "[u]nder these securities, the husband incurred an equally onerous potential liability in respect of any borrowings from the pursuer by the wife. Each spouse secured the debts of the other."[111]

A security therefore – apparently almost any "all sums" security granted jointly by husband and wife – contains a co-extensive obligation between the spouses that each stands as cautioner for any additional lending obtained from the lender by the other. Mrs Cooper clearly had no intention to borrow further from the bank, but the fact is that she could have, and Mr Cooper would have been liable to the extent of his interest in the family home.

To that extent it is possible to argue that few, if any, standard securities jointly granted by spouses could ever be gratuitous as there is almost always scope for one spouse to run up additional debt to the lender without the knowledge of the other and for that debt to be covered. Such reasoning may render *Smith* redundant, but this is a point which has thus far gone unargued.

Securities granted by only one spouse

The foregoing logic leads to a further potential area of exploration. All of the Smith type cases have so far dealt with securities granted by both spouses. There has so far been no serious consideration of the situation where one spouse owns the property and grants security. This would encompass situations like the Mumfords in the *Smith* case, where the spouse consents to the transaction due to his or her occupancy rights as well as situations where a wife owns property in her sole name and is persuaded to grant security over it for her husband's business.

Many of the foregoing principles would apply to the latter case, but it is an interesting question whether a spouse with only statutory occupancy rights could truly be covered by *Smith*.

---

[111] 2004 SC 153 at p.159

Further consideration by the Supreme Court?

Almost incredibly, despite multiple actions having reached the Inner House of the Court of Session, *Smith* remains the only House of Lords/Supreme Court authority in this area in Scotland. Given the further development of the law by the House in England and Wales, and the stated aim of the Court in keeping the law of Scotland broadly in line with the law of England in this area, it is perhaps odd that the matter has not gone back before the highest court in the land.

It is known that several litigants have considered taking that step. Indeed the Wilsons did appeal to the Supreme Court following their defeat at the Inner House. Whilst they were successful in the appeal, it was on grounds which had nothing whatever to do with the *Smith* principle.[112]

Whilst the side-stepping of the point by the Supreme Court in *Wilson* may tell its own story, there is no doubt that the post-*Smith* jurisprudence has created a gulf between the law of Scotland and the law of England and Wales in an area where the House of Lords were specifically seeking unity. It is therefore very much a live possibility that the right case brought before the Supreme Court might result in a readjustment of the accepted position and the adoption of something closer to the *Etridge (No.2)* principles into the law of Scotland.

---

112 See *Royal Bank of Scotland plc -v- Wilson* 2011 SC (UKSC) 66 – the case did have a profound effect on the process followed by lenders seeking to take possession of properties, which is beyond the scope of this book.

MORE BOOKS BY LAW BRIEF PUBLISHING

‘Covid-19, Homeworking and the Law – The Essential Guide to Employment and GDPR Issues’ by Forbes Solicitors
‘Covid-19, Force Majeure and Frustration of Contracts – The Essential Guide’ by Keith Markham
‘Covid-19 and Criminal Law – The Essential Guide’ by Ramya Nagesh
‘Covid-19 and Family Law in England and Wales – The Essential Guide’ by Safda Mahmood
‘A Practical Guide to the Law of Unlawful Eviction and Harassment – 2nd Edition’ by Stephanie Lovegrove
‘Covid-19, Residential Property, Equity Release and Enfranchisement – The Essential Guide’ by Paul Sams and Louise Uphill
‘Covid-19, Brexit and the Law of Commercial Leases – The Essential Guide’ by Mark Shelton
‘A Practical Guide to Costs in Personal Injury Claims – 2nd Edition’ by Matthew Hoe
‘A Practical Guide to the General Data Protection Regulation (GDPR) – 2nd Edition’ by Keith Markham
‘Ellis on Credit Hire – Sixth Edition’ by Aidan Ellis & Tim Kevan
‘A Practical Guide to Working with Litigants in Person and McKenzie Friends in Family Cases’ by Stuart Barlow
‘Protecting Unregistered Brands: A Practical Guide to the Law of Passing Off’ by Lorna Brazell
‘A Practical Guide to Secondary Liability and Joint Enterprise Post-Jogee’ by Joanne Cecil & James Mehigan
‘A Practical Guide to the Pre-Action RTA Claims Protocol for Personal Injury Lawyers’ by Antonia Ford
‘A Practical Guide to Neighbour Disputes and the Law’ by Alexander Walsh
‘A Practical Guide to Forfeiture of Leases’ by Mark Shelton
‘A Practical Guide to Coercive Control for Legal Practitioners and Victims’ by Rachel Horman

'A Practical Guide to Rights Over Airspace and Subsoil' by Daniel Gatty
'Tackling Disclosure in the Criminal Courts – A Practitioner's Guide' by Narita Bahra QC & Don Ramble
'A Practical Guide to the Law of Driverless Cars – Second Edition' by Alex Glassbrook, Emma Northey & Scarlett Milligan
'A Practical Guide to TOLATA Claims' by Greg Williams
'Artificial Intelligence – The Practical Legal Issues' by John Buyers
'A Practical Guide to the Law of Prescription in Scotland' by Andrew Foyle
'A Practical Guide to the Construction and Rectification of Wills and Trust Instruments' by Edward Hewitt
'A Practical Guide to the Law of Bullying and Harassment in the Workplace' by Philip Hyland
'How to Be a Freelance Solicitor: A Practical Guide to the SRA-Regulated Freelance Solicitor Model' by Paul Bennett
'A Practical Guide to Prison Injury Claims' by Malcolm Johnson
'A Practical Guide to the Small Claims Track' by Dominic Bright
'A Practical Guide to Advising Clients at the Police Station' by Colin Stephen McKeown-Beaumont
'A Practical Guide to Antisocial Behaviour Injunctions' by Iain Wightwick
'Practical Mediation: A Guide for Mediators, Advocates, Advisers, Lawyers, and Students in Civil, Commercial, Business, Property, Workplace, and Employment Cases' by Jonathan Dingle with John Sephton
'The Mini-Pupillage Workbook' by David Boyle
'A Practical Guide to Crofting Law' by Brian Inkster
'A Practical Guide to Spousal Maintenance' by Liz Cowell
'A Practical Guide to the Law of Domain Names and Cybersquatting' by Andrew Clemson
'A Practical Guide to the Law of Gender Pay Gap Reporting' by Harini Iyengar

‘A Practical Guide to the Rights of Grandparents in Children Proceedings’ by Stuart Barlow

‘NHS Whistleblowing and the Law’ by Joseph England

‘Employment Law and the Gig Economy’ by Nigel Mackay & Annie Powell

‘A Practical Guide to Noise Induced Hearing Loss (NIHL) Claims’ by Andrew Mckie, Ian Skeate, Gareth McAloon

‘An Introduction to Beauty Negligence Claims – A Practical Guide for the Personal Injury Practitioner’ by Greg Almond

‘Intercompany Agreements for Transfer Pricing Compliance’ by Paul Sutton

‘Zen and the Art of Mediation’ by Martin Plowman

‘A Practical Guide to the SRA Principles, Individual and Law Firm Codes of Conduct 2019 – What Every Law Firm Needs to Know’ by Paul Bennett

‘A Practical Guide to Adoption for Family Lawyers’ by Graham Pegg

‘A Practical Guide to Industrial Disease Claims’ by Andrew Mckie & Ian Skeate

‘A Practical Guide to Redundancy’ by Philip Hyland

‘A Practical Guide to Vicarious Liability’ by Mariel Irvine

‘A Practical Guide to Applications for Landlord’s Consent and Variation of Leases’ by Mark Shelton

‘A Practical Guide to Relief from Sanctions Post-Mitchell and Denton’ by Peter Causton

‘A Practical Guide to Equity Release for Advisors’ by Paul Sams

‘A Practical Guide to the Law Relating to Food’ by Ian Thomas

‘A Practical Guide to Financial Services Claims’ by Chris Hegarty

‘The Law of Houses in Multiple Occupation: A Practical Guide to HMO Proceedings’ by Julian Hunt

‘A Practical Guide to Unlawful Eviction and Harassment’ by Stephanie Lovegrove

‘Occupiers, Highways and Defective Premises Claims: A Practical Guide Post-Jackson – 2nd Edition’ by Andrew Mckie

www.ingramcontent.com/pod-product-compliance
Lightning Source LLC
LaVergne TN
LVHW022303200926
848481LV00004B/1201